Atlas of Sustainable Development Goals

2018 From World Development Indicators

WORLD BANK GROUP

Foreword

The 17 Sustainable Development Goals (SDGs) represent the world's most ambitious plan to promote the sustainable development of our people and planet—and are fully aligned with the World Bank Group's twin goals to end extreme poverty and build shared prosperity in a sustainable manner.

Achieving the SDGs by 2030 will require more and better financing, a renewed focus on implementation to improve the lives of those hardest to reach, and significant improvements in data collection and analysis.

The World Bank Group's country-led processes have shown us that countries have a strong desire to meet the objectives of the 2030 Agenda, and as a result, our support for this work continues to grow. The professionals in our sectoral global practices already possess deep knowledge of and experience in regard to all 17 of the SDGs.

That expertise is reflected in this *Atlas of Sustainable Development Goals 2018*, which presents a visual guide to key trends and the issues that surround them. It aims to help us better understand progress on the SDGs and to aid policy makers engaging with them in their everyday work.

This *Atlas* would not be possible without the efforts of statisticians and data scientists working in national and international agencies around the world. By quantifying our work, they help shape development interventions and approaches so that we can all make better decisions about our lives and the resources we manage.

The *Atlas* draws on the World Bank Group's *World Development Indicators*, a database of more than 1,400 indicators for more than 220 economies, many going back over 50 years. It also explores new data from scientists and researchers where standards for measuring SDG targets are still being developed.

Data are critical for decision making and accountability. While analysis of big data is commonplace in the private sector, similar techniques can be adopted by development professionals to gain real-time insights into people's well-being and to better target aid interventions for vulnerable groups.

Ultimately, the purpose of managing data in this way is to produce measurable results—improved resilience to economic, environmental, and humanitarian shocks; more jobs and opportunities; and improved education, health, nutrition, and gender equality—while leaving no one behind.

The SDGs have energized our efforts to work with partners to reach these ambitious targets—and this *Atlas* provides the type of knowledge we need to most efficiently direct our efforts to achieve them.

Mahmoud Mohieldin
Senior Vice President
World Bank Group

Acknowledgments

The *Atlas of Sustainable Development Goals 2018* was produced by the Development Economics Data Group of the World Bank, in collaboration with the Global Practices and Cross-Cutting Solution Areas of the World Bank and the Office of the Senior Vice President for the 2030 Development Agenda, United Nations Relations, and Partnerships.

The publication was prepared by a team led by Tariq Khokhar and Andrew Whitby, under the management of Umar Serajuddin and the overall direction of Haishan Fu. The maps and data visualizations were produced by Meera Desai, Tariq Khokhar, Karthik Ramanathan Dhanalakshmi Ramanathan, and Andrew Whitby.

Elizabeth Purdie managed the editorial process, and contributions were received from Husein Abdul-Hamid, Paola Agostini, Luis Alberto Andres, Saniya Ansar, Raka Banerjee, Daron Bedrosyan, Juliette Besnard, Hasita Bhammar, Randall Brummett, Ana Elisa Bucher, Eliana Carranza, Simon Davies, Klaus Deininger, Harun Dogo, Vivien Foster, Alvaro Gonzalez, Stephanie Hallegatte, Ellen Hamilton, Nagaraja Rao Harshadeep, Lewis Hawke, Tim Herzog, Barbro Hexeberg, Thea Hilhorst, Masako Hiraga, Patrick Hoang-Vu Eozenou, Aira Maria Htenas, Atsushi Iimi, Oleksiy Ivaschenko, Chris Jackson, Arvind Jain, Filip Jolevski, Bala Bhaskar Naidu Kalimili, Haruna Kashiwase, Buyant Khaltarkhuu, Tariq Khokhar, Silvia Kirova, Leora Klapper, Charles Kouame, Jens Kristensen, Craig P. Kullmann, Yunziyi Lang, Samuel Lantei Mills, Jia Jun Lee, Joseph Lemoine, Shiqing Li, Libbet Loughnan, Hiroko Maeda, David Mariano, Dino Merotto, Ines Mugica, Silvia Muzi, Petra Nahmias, Esther Naikal, Marco Nicoli, Marina Novikova, Tigran Parvanyan, Oya Pinar Ardic Alper, Ana Florina Pirlea, Tanya Primiani, Espen Beer Prydz, Elizabeth Purdie, Kanta Rigaud, David A. Robalino, Claudia Rodriguez Alas, Jorge Rodriguez Meza, Eliana Carolina Rubiano Matulevich, Evis Rucaj, Fernanda Ruiz Nunez, Valentina Saltane, Umar Serajuddin, Dorothe Singer, Avjeet Singh, Danett Song, Rubena Sukaj, Emi Suzuki, Siv Elin Tokle, Wendy Ven-dee Huang, Michael Weber, Andrew Whitby, Dereje Wolde, Elisson Wright, Yi Xu, and Urska Zrinski.

Guidance and comments were provided by the Office of the Senior Vice President for the 2030 Development Agenda, United Nations Relations, and Partnerships, particularly Farida Aboulmagd, Mike Kelleher, and Marco Scuriatti. The report benefited from comments and suggestions from David Rosenblatt of the Development Economics Operations and Strategy Unit.

Bruno Bonansea provided guidance on maps. Michael Harrup, Jewel McFadden, and Yaneisy Martinez oversaw printing and distribution. A team at Communications Development Incorporated—led by Bruce Ross-Larson and including Joe Caponio, Christopher Trott, and Elaine Wilson—managed the design, editing, and layout. Jomo Tariku managed the print and digital publication process, designed the cover, and produced promotional materials with David Mariano. Lisa Burke provided administrative support. Malarvizhi Veerappan led the systems team managing data from which much of this publication draws.

The authors are grateful to the communities behind the multiple open-source software packages used to develop this publication. In particular, the authors relied heavily on the R statistical computing environment, the ggplot2 data visualization library, and the QGIS geographic information system software.

About the Atlas

The *Atlas of Sustainable Development Goals 2018* presents maps, charts, and stories related to the Sustainable Development Goals (SDGs). It discusses trends, comparisons, and measurement issues using accessible and shareable data visualizations.

The data draw on the World Development Indicators (WDI) database—the World Bank's compilation of internationally comparable statistics about global development and the quality of people's lives. For each of the SDGs, relevant indicators have been chosen to illustrate important ideas.

In some cases—for example, those in which country or temporal coverage is limited—supplementary data from other databases or published studies have been used. For some targets, there may be no reliable data to use for comparisons between countries or to measure progress.

The cutoff date for data included in this edition is March 30, 2018.

The 2018 *Atlas* uses two primary methods for classifying and aggregating countries and economies—by income (as defined for the World Bank's 2018 fiscal year) and by region. These are presented in the maps on pages viii–xi.

For more information, including details on the structure of the coding scheme; the methodology, concepts, definitions, coverage, periodicity, and development relevance of all WDI indicators; and the methods used for classifying countries for analytical purposes, please refer to http://datahelpdesk.worldbank.org

All the figures in this *Atlas* are produced in R with ggplot2 or with QGIS. For a digital version of this publication and the source code for the majority of charts and maps, please refer to http://data.worldbank.org/sdgatlas

Example: Despite its importance, enrollment in pre-primary education is not universal.

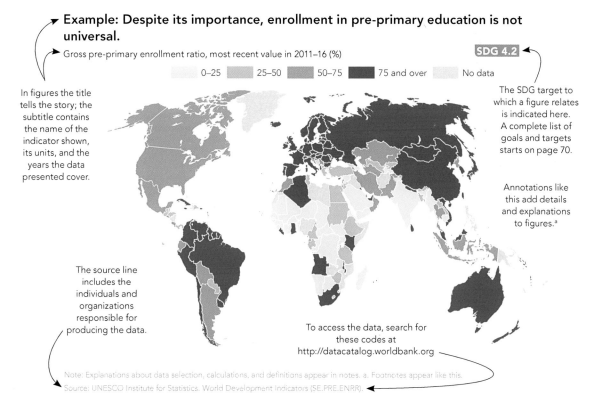

Gross pre-primary enrollment ratio, most recent value in 2011–16 (%)

SDG 4.2

0–25   25–50   50–75   75 and over   No data

In figures the title tells the story; the subtitle contains the name of the indicator shown, its units, and the years the data presented cover.

The SDG target to which a figure relates is indicated here. A complete list of goals and targets starts on page 70.

Annotations like this add details and explanations to figures.[a]

The source line includes the individuals and organizations responsible for producing the data.

To access the data, search for these codes at http://datacatalog.worldbank.org

Note: Explanations about data selection, calculations, and definitions appear in notes. a. Footnotes appear like this.

Source: UNESCO Institute for Statistics. World Development Indicators (SE.PRE.ENRR).

Introduction

The World Bank is one of the world's largest producers of development data and research. But our responsibility does not stop with making these global public goods available; we need to make them understandable to a general audience. When both the public and policy makers share an evidence-based view of the world, real advances in social and economic development, such as achieving the Sustainable Development Goals (SDGs), become possible.

This *Atlas of Sustainable Development Goals 2018* is a visual guide to the data on each of the 17 SDGs. With more than 180 annotated charts and maps, it presents this information in a way that is easy to browse, share, teach, and understand.

You'll see both progress and possibility. Life expectancy has risen around the world since the 1960s, but even today, in low-income countries a third of all deaths are among children under age 5. New data show that only 69 percent of the world's adults have an account with a financial institution or mobile money provider, and they're even less likely to have an account if they're women, younger, poorer, or less educated.

The *Atlas* draws on *World Development Indicators* but also incorporates data from other sources. For example, research by Global Fishing Watch analyzes radio transmissions used by industrial fishing vessels for collision detection to show the most heavily fished regions of the ocean and the impact humans are having on those ecosystems. The *Atlas* moves beyond averages and features local and disaggregated data. For instance, the discussion of air pollution presents national estimates for most countries, a subnational view showing variations within large countries such as China and India, and a year-long view showing a city's seasonal variation in pollution picked up by one sensor at Delhi Technological University.

Given the breadth and scope of the SDGs, the *Atlas* is selective, emphasizing issues considered important by subject experts, data scientists, and statisticians at the World Bank.

The foundation for any evidence is trust: trust that data have been collected, managed, and analyzed responsibly and trust that they have been faithfully presented. The *Atlas* is the first World Bank publication that sets out to be computationally reproducible—the majority of its charts and maps are produced with published code, directly from public data sources such as the World Bank's Open Data platform.

The *Atlas* distills the World Bank's knowledge of data related to the SDGs. I hope it inspires you to explore these issues further so that we can collectively accelerate progress toward achieving the SDGs.

Shanta Devarajan
Senior Director, Development Economics and
Acting Chief Economist
World Bank Group

Contents

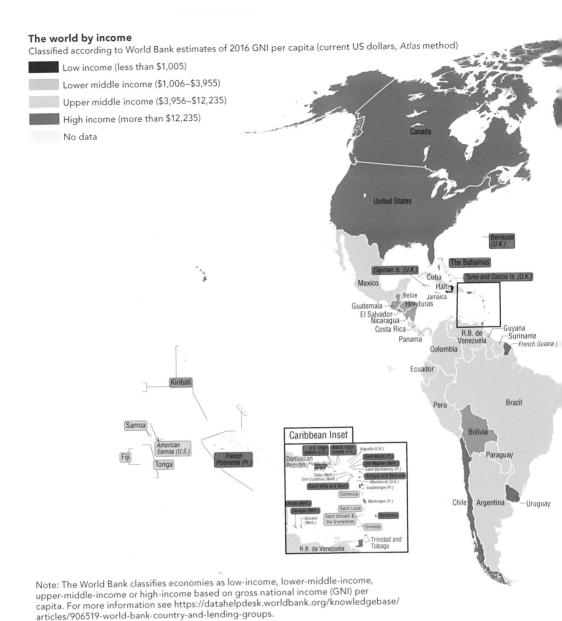

The world by income
Classified according to World Bank estimates of 2016 GNI per capita (current US dollars, *Atlas* method)

- Low income (less than $1,005)
- Lower middle income ($1,006–$3,955)
- Upper middle income ($3,956–$12,235)
- High income (more than $12,235)
- No data

Note: The World Bank classifies economies as low-income, lower-middle-income, upper-middle-income or high-income based on gross national income (GNI) per capita. For more information see https://datahelpdesk.worldbank.org/knowledgebase/articles/906519-world-bank-country-and-lending-groups.

East Asia and Pacific

American Samoa	Upper middle income
Australia	High income
Brunei Darussalam	High income
Cambodia	Lower middle income
China	Upper middle income
Fiji	Upper middle income
French Polynesia	High income
Guam	High income
Hong Kong SAR, China	High income
Indonesia	Lower middle income
Japan	High income
Kiribati	Lower middle income
Korea, Dem. People's Rep.	Low income
Korea, Rep.	High income
Lao PDR	Lower middle income
Macao SAR, China	High income
Malaysia	Upper middle income
Marshall Islands	Upper middle income
Micronesia, Fed. Sts.	Lower middle income
Mongolia	Lower middle income
Myanmar	Lower middle income
Nauru	Upper middle income
New Caledonia	High income
New Zealand	High income
Northern Mariana Islands	High income
Palau	High income
Papua New Guinea	Lower middle income
Philippines	Lower middle income
Samoa	Upper middle income
Singapore	High income
Solomon Islands	Lower middle income
Thailand	Upper middle income
Timor-Leste	Lower middle income
Tonga	Upper middle income
Tuvalu	Upper middle income
Vanuatu	Lower middle income
Vietnam	Lower middle income

Europe and Central Asia

Albania	Upper middle income
Andorra	High income
Armenia	Lower middle income
Austria	High income
Azerbaijan	Upper middle income
Belarus	Upper middle income
Belgium	High income
Bosnia and Herzegovina	Upper middle income
Bulgaria	Upper middle income
Channel Islands	High income
Croatia	Upper middle income
Cyprus	High income
Czech Republic	High income
Denmark	High income
Estonia	High income
Faroe Islands	High income
Finland	High income
France	High income

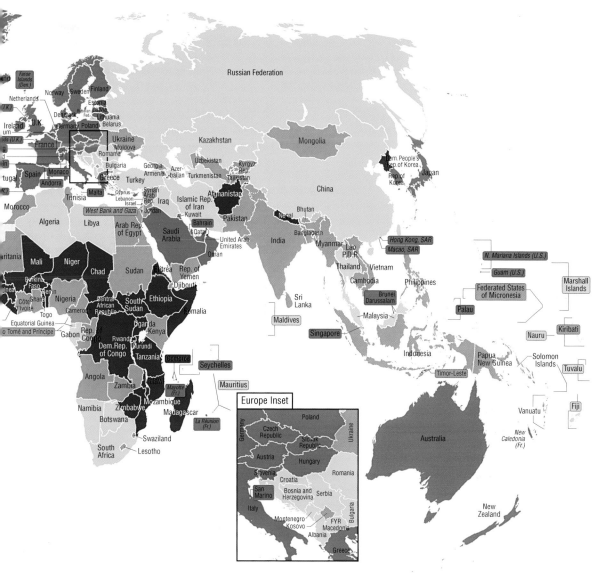

Atlas of Sustainable Development Goals 2018

Georgia	Lower middle income	Montenegro	Upper middle income	**Latin America and the Caribbean**
Germany	High income	Netherlands	High income	**Antigua and Barbuda** High income
Gibraltar	High income	Norway	High income	**Argentina** Upper middle income
Greece	High income	Poland	High income	**Aruba** High income
Greenland	High income	Portugal	High income	**Bahamas, The** High income
Hungary	High income	Romania	Upper middle income	**Barbados** High income
Iceland	High income	Russian Federation	Upper middle income	**Belize** Upper middle income
Ireland	High income	San Marino	High income	**Bolivia** Lower middle income
Isle of Man	High income	Serbia	Upper middle income	**Brazil** Upper middle income
Italy	High income	Slovak Republic	High income	**British Virgin Islands** High income
Kazakhstan	Upper middle income	Slovenia	High income	**Cayman Islands** High income
Kosovo	Lower middle income	Spain	High income	**Chile** High income
Kyrgyz Republic	Lower middle income	Sweden	High income	**Colombia** Upper middle income
Latvia	High income	Switzerland	High income	**Costa Rica** Upper middle income
Liechtenstein	High income	Tajikistan	Lower middle income	**Cuba** Upper middle income
Lithuania	High income	Turkey	Upper middle income	**Curaçao** High income
Luxembourg	High income	Turkmenistan	Upper middle income	**Dominica** Upper middle income
Macedonia, FYR	Upper middle income	Ukraine	Lower middle income	**Dominican Republic** Upper middle income
Moldova	Lower middle income	United Kingdom	High income	**Ecuador** Upper middle income
Monaco	High income	Uzbekistan	Lower middle income	**El Salvador** Lower middle income

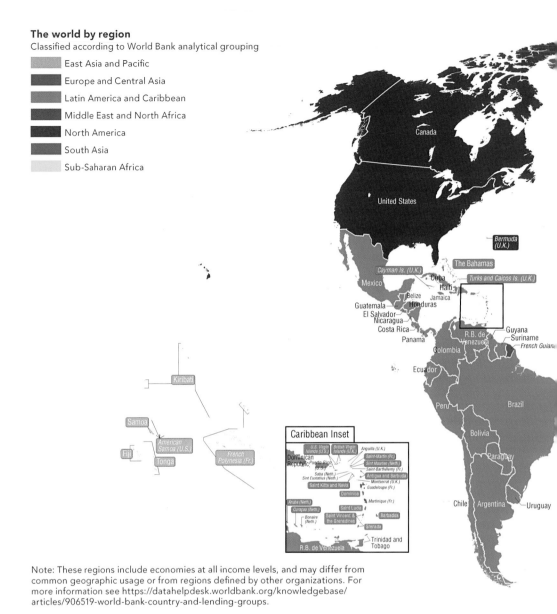

The world by region

Classified according to World Bank analytical grouping

- East Asia and Pacific
- Europe and Central Asia
- Latin America and Caribbean
- Middle East and North Africa
- North America
- South Asia
- Sub-Saharan Africa

Canada

United States

Bermuda (U.K.)

Cayman Is. (U.K.)
The Bahamas
Cuba
Turks and Caicos Is. (U.K.)
Mexico
Haiti
Belize
Jamaica
Guatemala
Honduras
El Salvador
Nicaragua
Costa Rica
Panama
R.B. de Venezuela
Guyana
Suriname
French Guiana
Colombia
Ecuador
Peru
Brazil
Bolivia
Paraguay
Chile
Argentina
Uruguay

Kiribati

Samoa
American Samoa (U.S.)
Fiji
Tonga
French Polynesia (Fr.)

Caribbean Inset

U.S. Virgin Islands (U.S.)
British Virgin Islands (U.K.)
Anguilla (U.K.)
Saint-Martin (Fr.)
Dominican Republic
Puerto Rico (U.S.)
Sint Maarten (Neth.)
Saint-Barthélemy (Fr.)
Saba (Neth.)
Sint Eustatius (Neth.)
Antigua and Barbuda
Montserrat (U.K.)
Saint Kitts and Nevis
Guadeloupe (Fr.)
Dominica
Aruba (Neth.)
Martinique (Fr.)
Curaçao (Neth.)
Saint Lucia
Bonaire (Neth.)
Saint Vincent & the Grenadines
Barbados
Grenada
R.B. de Venezuela
Trinidad and Tobago

Note: These regions include economies at all income levels, and may differ from common geographic usage or from regions defined by other organizations. For more information see https://datahelpdesk.worldbank.org/knowledgebase/articles/906519-world-bank-country-and-lending-groups.

Grenada	Upper middle income	Trinidad and Tobago	High income	Malta	High income
Guatemala	Lower middle income	Turks and Caicos Islands	High income	Morocco	Lower middle income
Guyana	Upper middle income			Oman	High income
Haiti	Low income	Uruguay	High income	Qatar	High income
Honduras	Lower middle income	Venezuela, RB	Upper middle income	Saudi Arabia	High income
Jamaica	Upper middle income	Virgin Islands (U.S.)	High income	Syrian Arab Republic	Lower middle income
Mexico	Upper middle income			Tunisia	Lower middle income
Nicaragua	Lower middle income	**Middle East and North Africa**		United Arab Emirates	High income
Panama	Upper middle income	Algeria	Upper middle income	West Bank and Gaza	Lower middle income
Paraguay	Upper middle income	Bahrain	High income	Yemen, Rep.	Lower middle income
Peru	Upper middle income	Djibouti	Lower middle income		
Puerto Rico	High income	Egypt, Arab Rep.	Lower middle income	**North America**	
Sint Maarten	High income	Iran, Islamic Rep.	Upper middle income	Bermuda	High income
St. Kitts and Nevis	High income	Iraq	Upper middle income	Canada	High income
St. Lucia	Upper middle income	Israel	High income	United States	High income
St. Martin	High income	Jordan	Lower middle income		
St. Vincent and the Grenadines	Upper middle income	Kuwait	High income	**South Asia**	
		Lebanon	Upper middle income	Afghanistan	Low income
Suriname	Upper middle income	Libya	Upper middle income	Bangladesh	Lower middle income

Populous countries such as China, India, Indonesia, and Bangladesh are home to a significant share of the total number of people living in extreme poverty.

Number of people living on less than $1.90 a day (2011 PPP), most recent value in 2010–13 (millions)

SDG 1.1

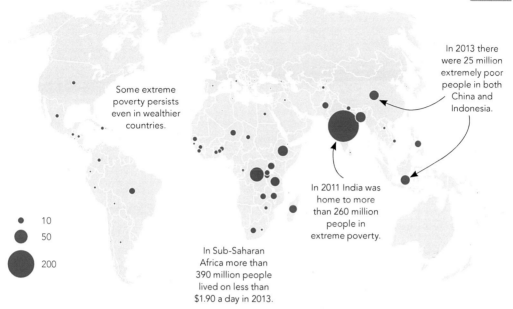

Some extreme poverty persists even in wealthier countries.

In 2013 there were 25 million extremely poor people in both China and Indonesia.

In 2011 India was home to more than 260 million people in extreme poverty.

In Sub-Saharan Africa more than 390 million people lived on less than $1.90 a day in 2013.

10
50
200

Source: World Bank PovcalNet. World Development Indicators (SI.POV.DDAY; SP.POP.TOTL).

Poverty rates at national poverty lines are generally higher than at the international $1.90 a day line, and they are higher in rural areas than in urban areas.

Poverty headcount ratio, most recent value in 2010–15 (% of population)

SDG 1.2

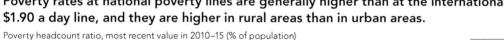

East Asia & Pacific   Latin America & Caribbean   South Asia
Europe & Central Asia   Middle East & North Africa   Sub-Saharan Africa

Poverty rate at national poverty lines

Rural poverty rate at national poverty lines

In countries on this side of the line, people living near $1.90 a day are not considered poor by national definitions.

In countries on this side of the line, poverty rates are higher in urban areas than in rural areas.

Poverty rate at $1.90 a day (2011 PPP)

Urban poverty rate at national poverty lines

Source: World Bank PovcalNet. World Development Indicators (SI.POV.DDAY; SI.POV.NAHC; SI.POV.RUHC; SI.POV.URHC).

Richer countries have more comprehensive social protection programs. Within countries the poorest are more likely to be covered by such programs, but targeting support toward the poor remains challenging.

Share of population covered by any social protection and labor program, most recent survey in 2008–16 (%)

SDG 1.3

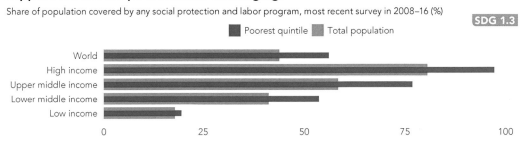

Poorest quintile   Total population

Note: Calculated using simple averages of country-level coverage rates across income groups. Actual coverage may be higher as not all programs are captured by household surveys in some countries. Poorest quintile is calculated using pre-transfer welfare (income or consumption) per capita.

Source: World Bank ASPIRE: Atlas of Social Protection Indicators of Resilience and Equity 2018. http://hdl.handle.net/10986/29115

The most common social protection programs in every region are cash based.

Share of spending on the social safety net, by program (%)

SDG 1.3

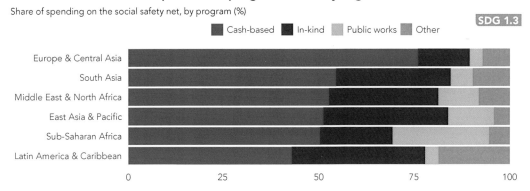

Cash-based   In-kind   Public works   Other

Note: Based on administrative data. Cash-based programs include universal cash transfers, conditional cash transfers, and social pensions. In-kind programs include school feeding, fee waivers and other in-kind transfers.

Source: World Bank ASPIRE: Atlas of Social Protection Indicators of Resilience and Equity 2018. http://hdl.handle.net/10986/29115

Cash transfer programs are the most likely to be directed toward the poor.

Share of social security programs benefiting each population quintile, most recent survey in 2008–16 (%)

SDG 1.3

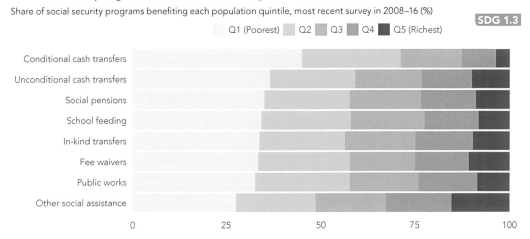

Q1 (Poorest)   Q2   Q3   Q4   Q5 (Richest)

Note: Calculated using simple averages of country-level coverage rates across regions. Poorest quintile is calculated using pre-transfer welfare (income or consumption) per capita.

Source: World Bank ASPIRE: Atlas of Social Protection Indicators of Resilience and Equity 2018. http://hdl.handle.net/10986/29115

Land rights provide security of tenure and are important for reducing poverty. But many countries lack a comprehensive land registry that records ownership.

Number of components related to property registration from Doing Business Index (0–4, higher is better)

0 1 2 3 4 No data

SDG 1.4

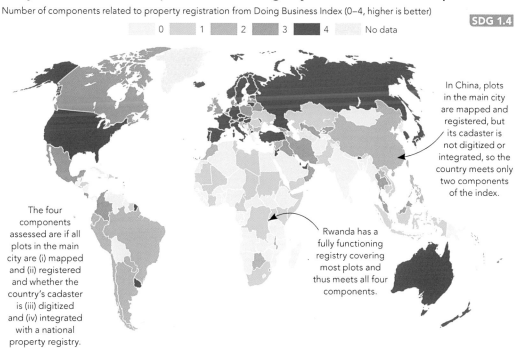

In China, plots in the main city are mapped and registered, but its cadaster is not digitized or integrated, so the country meets only two components of the index.

The four components assessed are if all plots in the main city are (i) mapped and (ii) registered and whether the country's cadaster is (iii) digitized and (iv) integrated with a national property registry.

Rwanda has a fully functioning registry covering most plots and thus meets all four components.

Source: World Bank Doing Business (database). http://www.doingbusiness.org

People with documented ownership of land and property feel more secure.

Share of households, most recent value in 2010–15 (%)

- Perceived tenure insecurity
- Own formally documented agricultural land

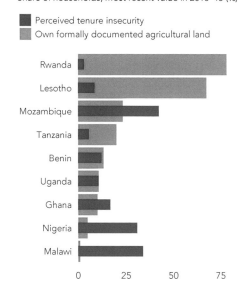

In some countries few women are documented on formal land titles.

Share of households that own agricultural land or houses, most recent value in 2001–15 (%)

SDG 1.4

- Female included on land title
- No female on land title
- No formal land title

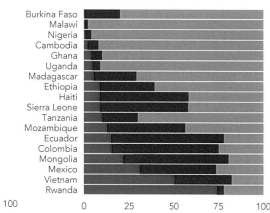

Note: Data from a study covering selected countries
Source: Carletto, Deininger, Hilhorst, and Zakout (2018).

Note: Data from a study covering selected countries.
Source: Carletto, Deininger, Hilhorst, and Zakout (2018).

Zero hunger

End hunger, achieve food security and improved nutrition and promote sustainable agriculture

Young children and infants are most vulnerable to the effects of malnutrition. Globally, over 95 million fewer children were stunted in 2016 than in 1990.

Number of children under age 5 that are stunted, height for age (millions)

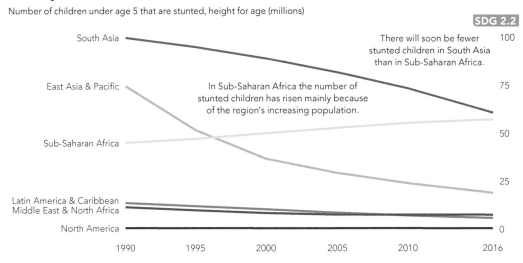

There will soon be fewer stunted children in South Asia than in Sub-Saharan Africa.

In Sub-Saharan Africa the number of stunted children has risen mainly because of the region's increasing population.

Note: Estimates not available for Europe & Central Asia due to poor data coverage.

Source: UNICEF, WHO and World Bank. WDI (SH.STA.STNT.ZS); Health Nutrition and Population Statistics (SP.POP.0004.FE; SP.POP.0004.MA).

Malnutrition is manifested in multiple ways. In lower-middle-income countries 12 percent of children suffer from wasting, while 5 percent are overweight.

Prevalence of different types of malnutrition, children under age 5, 2016 (%)

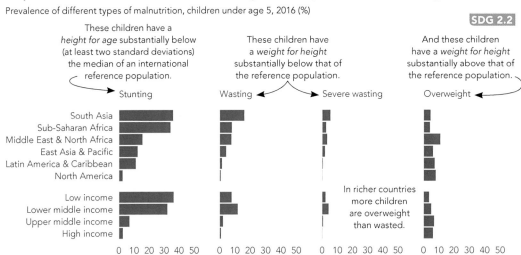

These children have a *height for age* substantially below (at least two standard deviations) the median of an international reference population.

These children have a *weight for height* substantially below that of the reference population.

And these children have a *weight for height* substantially above that of the reference population.

In richer countries more children are overweight than wasted.

Note: Regional aggregates for Europe & Central Asia are not available.

Source: UNICEF, WHO and World Bank. WDI (SH.STA.STNT.ZS; SH.STA.WAST.ZS; SH.SVR.WAST.ZS; SH.STA.OWGH.ZS).

There are large differences in stunting rates between rich & poor households...

Prevalence of stunting, children under age 5, most recent value in 2014–16 (%)

- ● Richest wealth quintile   ● Poorest wealth quintile

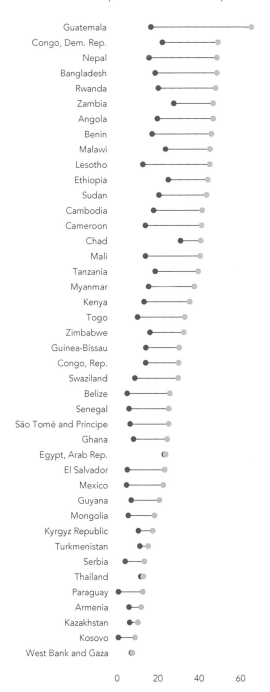

...and in many countries boys are more likely to be stunted than girls.

Prevalence of stunting, children under age 5, most recent value in 2012–15 (%)

SDG 2.2

- ● Female   ● Male

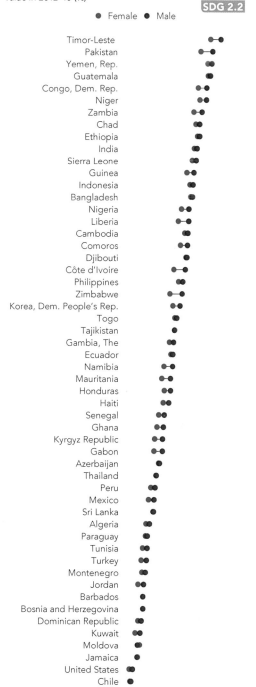

Source: UNICEF and The DHS Program, Health Nutrition and Population Statistics by Wealth Quintile (SH.STA.STNT.Q1.ZS; SH.STA.STNT.Q5.ZS)

Source: WHO, World Development Indicators (SH.STA.STNT.FE.ZS; SH.STA.STNT.MA.ZS).

Wasting affects 1 in 13 children globally. These 50 million children weigh less than expected for their height. Half of them live in South Asia, and a quarter live in Sub-Saharan Africa. Boys are more often affected than girls.

Prevalence of wasting, children under age 5, most recent value in 2005–15 (%)

SDG 2.2

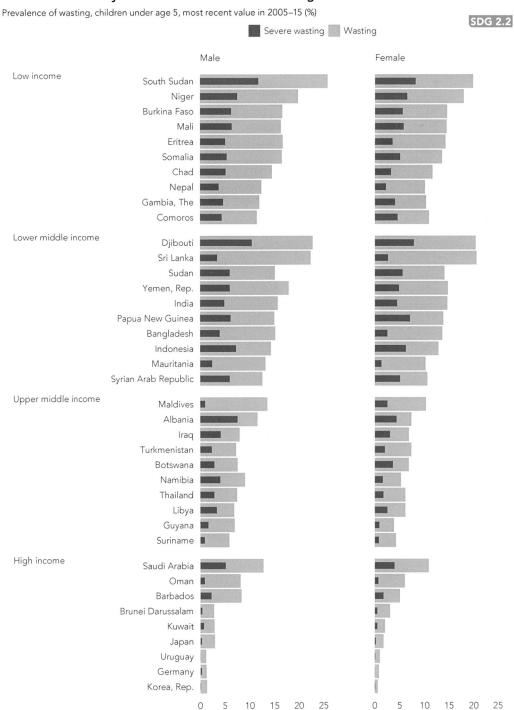

Note: For each income group, up to 10 countries with the highest average wasting rate and data available for both sexes are shown.
Source: UNICEF, WHO, and World Bank., WDI (SH.STA.WAST.MA.ZS; SH.SVR.WAST.MA.ZS; SH.STA.WAST.FE.ZS; SH.SVR.WAST.FE.ZS).

Globally, 1 in 10 people is undernourished and does not have enough food to meet his or her dietary needs. Undernourishment is most widespread in Sub-Saharan Africa, South Asia, and East Asia & Pacific.

Prevalence of undernourishment, 2015 (% of population)

SDG 2.1

0–5   5–15   15 and over   No data

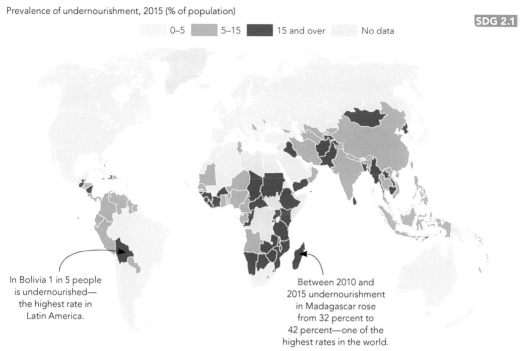

In Bolivia 1 in 5 people is undernourished—the highest rate in Latin America.

Between 2010 and 2015 undernourishment in Madagascar rose from 32 percent to 42 percent—one of the highest rates in the world.

Source: Food and Agriculture Organization. World Development Indicators (SN.ITK.DEFC.ZS).

The food deficit measures, on average, how much food people need to stop them from being considered undernourished. Food deficits have generally been declining but remain at levels at which many people lack sufficient calories.

Depth of the food deficit (kilocalories per person per day)

SDG 2.1

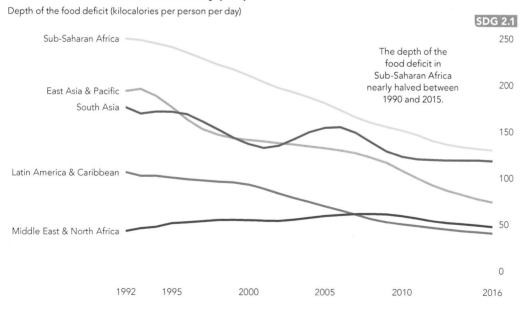

The depth of the food deficit in Sub-Saharan Africa nearly halved between 1990 and 2015.

Source: Food and Agriculture Organization. World Development Indicators (SN.ITK.DFCT).

Good health and well-being

Ensure healthy lives and promote well-being for all at all ages

3

Low-income countries have younger populations than high-income countries do. As countries become richer, fertility rates fall and life expectancy rises.

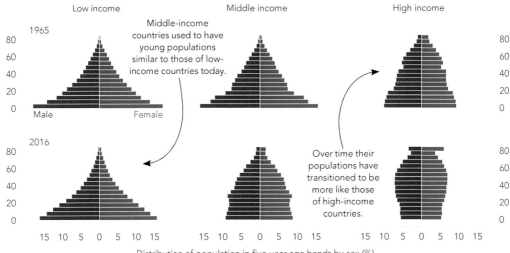

Distribution of population in five-year age bands by sex (%)

Note: Ages 80 and older are combined into a single group.

Source: World Bank and UN Population Division. World Development Indicators (SP.POP.0004.MA.5Y and other five-year bands by sex).

Demography is closely related to health outcomes: while life expectancy has generally risen, HIV/AIDS caused sharp declines in many countries in the 1990s.

Life expectancy at birth, by country (years)

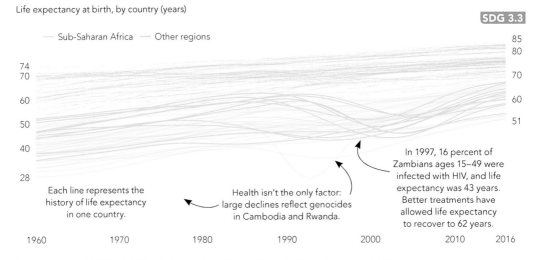

Note: The countries highlighted with heavier lines are those where all-time peak HIV prevalence exceeded 10 percent.

Source: UN Population Division and other sources. World Development Indicators (SP.DYN.LE00.IN).

In high-income countries the majority of people who die are old. But in low-income countries children under age 5 account for one in three deaths.

Deaths by sex and age group, 2010–15

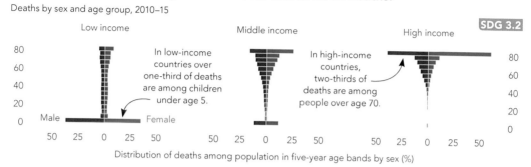

Low income   Middle income   High income

SDG 3.2

In low-income countries over one-third of deaths are among children under age 5.

In high-income countries, two-thirds of deaths are among people over age 70.

Male   Female

Distribution of deaths among population in five-year age bands by sex (%)

Note: Ages 80 and older are combined into a single group.

Source: UN Population Division, World Population Prospects 2017.

Children are at greatest risk in the first 28 days of life. Birth attendance by skilled health staff helps reduce maternal and neonatal mortality.

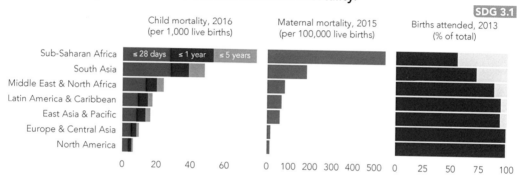

SDG 3.1

Child mortality, 2016
(per 1,000 live births)

Maternal mortality, 2015
(per 100,000 live births)

Births attended, 2013
(% of total)

Sub-Saharan Africa
South Asia
Middle East & North Africa
Latin America & Caribbean
East Asia & Pacific
Europe & Central Asia
North America

≤ 28 days   ≤ 1 year   ≤ 5 years

Source: UN Inter-agency Group for Child Mortality Estimation, WHO, UNICEF, UNFPA, World Bank, and UN Population Division. World Development Indicators (SH.DYN.NMRT; SP.DYN.IMRT.IN; SH.DYN.MORT; SH.STA.MMRT; SH.STA.BRTC.ZS).

Globally, 1 in 11 deaths is due to injury, and traffic accidents account for over a quarter of these. Over 1.25 million people died from road traffic injuries in 2015.

Mortality caused by road traffic injury, 2015 (per 100,000 people)

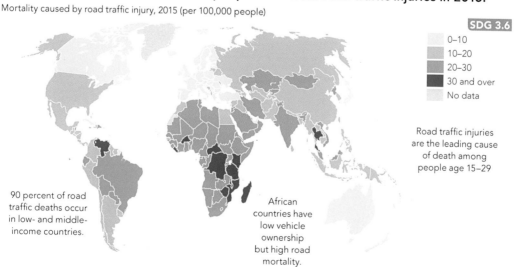

SDG 3.6

0–10
10–20
20–30
30 and over
No data

Road traffic injuries are the leading cause of death among people age 15–29

90 percent of road traffic deaths occur in low- and middle-income countries.

African countries have low vehicle ownership but high road mortality.

Source: WHO. World Development Indicators (SH.STA.TRAF.P5).

Not every country has enough health workers to meet the needs of its population. High-income countries have 15 times as many physicians as low-income countries do.

Physicians, nurses, and midwives, by country, most recent value in 2010–15 (per 1,000 people)

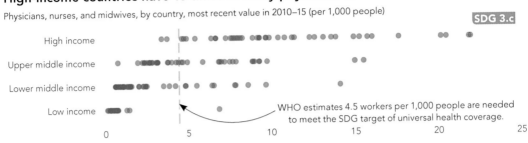

WHO estimates 4.5 workers per 1,000 people are needed to meet the SDG target of universal health coverage.

Source: WHO, OECD, and other sources. World Development Indicators (SH.MED.PHYS.ZS; SH.MED.NUMW.P3).

Low-income countries have a severe shortage of specialist surgical workers. All low- and most lower-middle-income countries have fewer than the target number.

Specialist surgical workforce, by country, most recent value in 2011–16 (per 100,000 people)

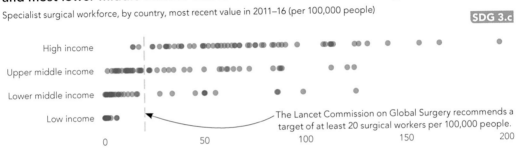

The Lancet Commission on Global Surgery recommends a target of at least 20 surgical workers per 100,000 people.

Source: The Lancet Commission on Global Surgery. World Development Indicators (SH.MED.SAOP.P5).

Better-staffed health systems can lead to improved health outcomes. For example, life expectancies are higher where there are more surgical workers per person.

Life expectancy at birth, by country, 2016 (years)

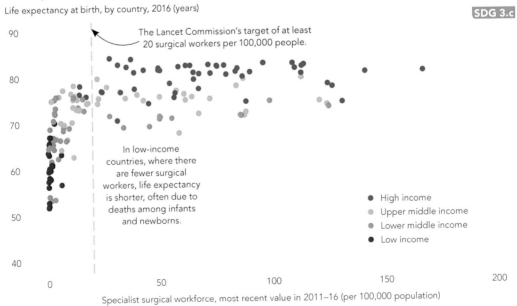

The Lancet Commission's target of at least 20 surgical workers per 100,000 people.

In low-income countries, where there are fewer surgical workers, life expectancy is shorter, often due to deaths among infants and newborns.

Specialist surgical workforce, most recent value in 2011–16 (per 100,000 population)

Source: The Lancet Commission on Global Surgery and UN Population Division. WDI (SH.MED.SAOP.P5; SP.DYN.LE00.IN).

Universal health coverage is about all people having access to the care they need without financial hardship. Service coverage varies widely across countries.

Universal Health Coverage service index, 2015

Under 50   50–60   60–70   70 and over   No data

SDG 3.8

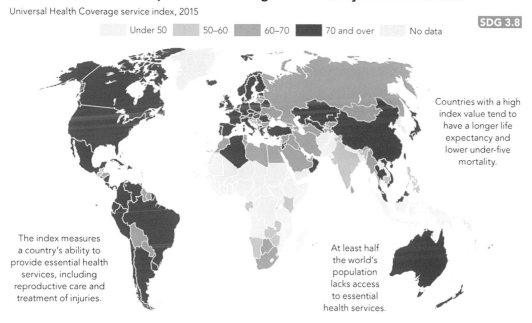

Countries with a high index value tend to have a longer life expectancy and lower under-five mortality.

The index measures a country's ability to provide essential health services, including reproductive care and treatment of injuries.

At least half the world's population lacks access to essential health services.

Source: Hogan and others. Universal Health Coverage (SH.UHC.SV.COV.IND).

In 2010, 800 million people spent over 10 percent of their household budget on healthcare, and 97 million were pushed into extreme poverty by health spending.

SDG 3.8

South Asia   Sub-Saharan Africa   Middle East & North Africa   North America
East Asia & Pacific   Latin America & Caribbean   Europe & Central Asia

People spending more than 10 percent of household consumption or income on out-of-pocket healthcare expenditure

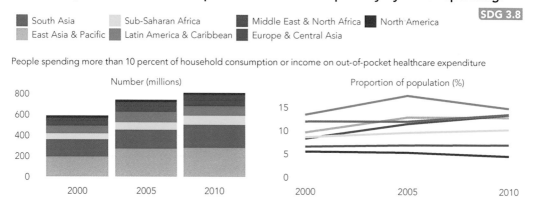

Number (millions)

Proportion of population (%)

Number of people pushed into poverty by out-of-pocket healthcare expenditure (millions)

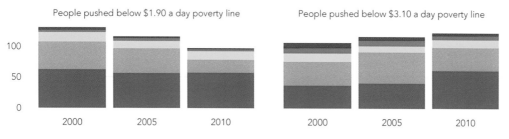

People pushed below $1.90 a day poverty line

People pushed below $3.10 a day poverty line

Source: Wagstaff and others. WDI (SH.UHC.NOP1.TO; SH.UHC.NOP2.TO; SH.UHC.OOPC.10.TO; SH.UHC.OOPC.10.ZS).

Quality education

4

Ensure inclusive and equitable quality education and promote lifelong learning opportunities for all

While most children are enrolled in primary education, fewer enroll at the secondary and tertiary levels.

Gross enrollment ratio, 2015 (%)

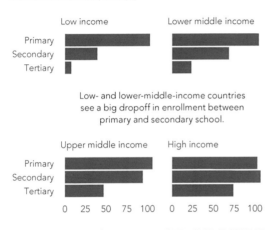

Low- and lower-middle-income countries see a big dropoff in enrollment between primary and secondary school.

Source: UNESCO Institute for Statistics. WDI (SE.PRM.ENRR; SE.SEC.ENRR; SE.TER.ENRR).

Not all children attend school at the right age, and so gross enrollment rates can exceed 100 percent.

Gross primary enrollment ratio, 2015 (%)

SDG 4.1

■ Correct age for school year ■ Older or younger

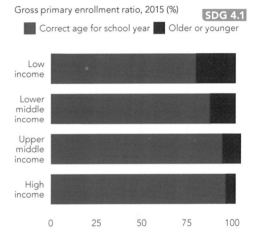

Source: UNESCO Institute for Statistics. WDI (SE.PRM.ENRR; SE.PRM.NENR).

Despite its importance, enrollment in pre-primary education is not universal.

Gross pre-primary enrollment ratio, most recent value in 2011–16 (%)

SDG 4.2

0–25 ■ 25–50 ■ 50–75 ■ 75 and over ■ No data

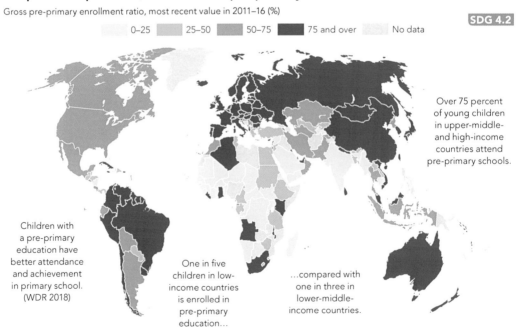

Over 75 percent of young children in upper-middle- and high-income countries attend pre-primary schools.

Children with a pre-primary education have better attendance and achievement in primary school. (WDR 2018)

One in five children in low-income countries is enrolled in pre-primary education...

...compared with one in three in lower-middle-income countries.

Source: UNESCO Institute for Statistics. World Development Indicators (SE.PRE.ENRR).

Education is an investment. All governments bear some responsibility for funding education; median spending on education worldwide is 5 percent of GDP.

Government spending on education, by country and regional median, most recent value in 2011–16 (% of GDP)

Note: Excludes Micronesia which is an outlier. Middle East & North Africa median value is from 2008.
Source: UNESCO Institute for Statistics, World Development Indicators (SE.XPD.TOTL.GD.ZS).

Many primary schools in Sub-Saharan Africa lack access to basic facilities that support learning, and many children are taught by teachers without qualifications.

Primary schools with access to facilities, and trained teachers, most recent value in 2010–14 (%)

SDG 4.a
SDG 4.c

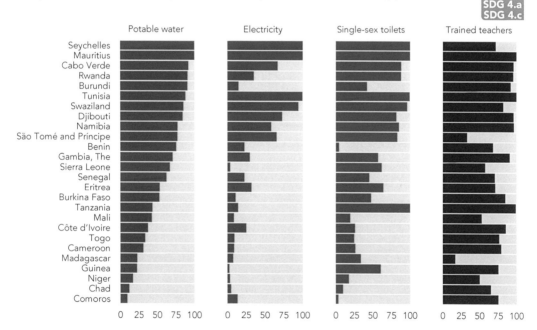

Note: Dataset limited to Sub-Saharan Africa. Only countries with data on all four dimensions shown.
Source: UNESCO Institute for Statistics, EdStats, and World Development Indicators (UIS.AFR.SCHBSP.1.PU.WELEC; UIS.AFR.SCHBSP.1.PU.WSTOIL; UIS.AFR.SCHBSP.1.PU.WPOWAT; SE.PRM.TCAQ.ZS).

Large class sizes are common in low- and lower-middle-income countries.

Average number of pupils per teacher, 2015

SDG 4.c

● High income ● Upper middle income ● Lower middle income ● Low income

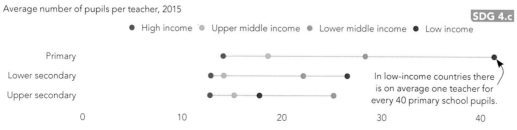

In low-income countries there is on average one teacher for every 40 primary school pupils.

Source: UNESCO Institute for Statistics, World Development Indicators (SE.PRM.ENRL.TC.ZS; SE.SEC.ENRL.LO.TC.ZS; SE.SEC.ENRL.UP.TC.ZS).

Gender gaps in early education completion have closed, except in low-income countries, where completion rates are about 5 percentage points higher for boys.

Completion rate (% of relevant age group)

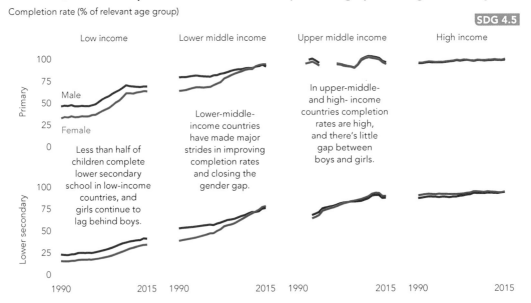

Source: UNESCO Institute for Statistics. WDI (SE.PRM.CMPT.MA.ZS; SE.PRM.CMPT.FE.ZS; SE.SEC.CMPT.LO.MA.ZS; SE.SEC.CMPT.LO.FE.ZS).

The relative share of male and female students enrolled in education varies substantially between countries, especially at the tertiary level.

Gender parity index (GPI) in gross school enrollment, by country, 2015

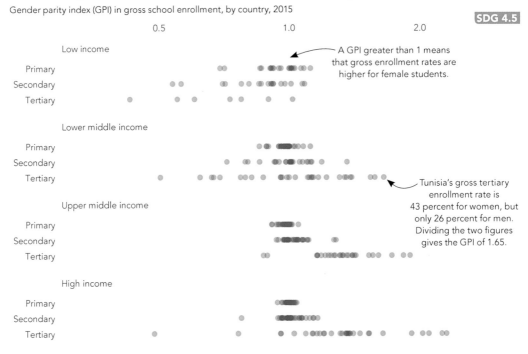

Note: Qatar's tertiary GPI of 6.95 is excluded as an outlier because of the large share of men in the general population.

Source: UNESCO Institute for Statistics. World Development Indicators (SE.ENR.PRIM.FM.ZS; SE.ENR.SECO.FM.ZS; SE.ENR.TERT.FM.ZS).

Girls enrolled in school are less likely to become pregnant as teenagers. Between 1990 and 2014 every region saw an increase in the share of girls enrolled in secondary school and a decline in adolescent fertility rates.

Adolescent fertility rate, by country (births per 1,000 women ages 15–19)

Adolescent fertility rate, by region, 1990–2014 (births per 1,000 women ages 15–19)

While higher rates of school enrollment are correlated with lower fertility rates, other factors such as access to contraception and lower child mortality also play a role.

In Sub-Saharan Africa enrollment rates doubled between 1990 and 2015, and the adolescent fertility rate fell by 25 percent.

In South Asia enrollment rates doubled, and the fertility rate fell by 65 percent.

Gross secondary school enrollment, female (%)

Source: UN Population Division and UNESCO Institute for Statistics. World Development Indicators (SE.SEC.ENRR.FE; SP.ADO.TFRT).

Gender equality

Achieve gender equality and empower all women and girls

Laws are a first step in helping women and girls achieve gender equality. About half of all countries have laws against gender-based discrimination in hiring.

Does the law mandate nondiscrimination based on gender in hiring? 2017

SDG 5.1
SDG 5.c

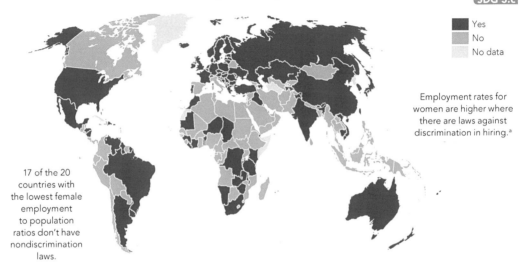

- Yes
- No
- No data

17 of the 20 countries with the lowest female employment to population ratios don't have nondiscrimination laws.

Employment rates for women are higher where there are laws against discrimination in hiring.[a]

a. World Bank Women, Business and the Law 2018.
Source: World Bank Women, Business and the Law 2018; World Development Indicators (SG.LAW.NODC.HR; SL.EMP.TOTL.SP.FE.ZS).

Laws may help protect women from violence, but two out of five countries have no clear penalties for domestic violence.

Are there clear criminal penalties for domestic violence? 2017

SDG 5.2

- Yes
- No
- No data

Despite penalties existing in Kiribati, the Solomon Islands, and Vanuatu, about 40 percent of women in these countries report violence from an intimate partner.

In Afghanistan, where there are no penalties, over 45 percent of women reported violence from an intimate partner.

Source: World Bank Women, Business and the Law 2018; World Development Indicators (SG.VAW.1549.ZS).

Although the legal age of marriage is 18 in most countries, a large share of women are married at an earlier age.

Age at first marriage, most recent value in 2008–16 (% of women ages 20–24)

SDG 5.3

■ 15 or younger ■ Between 15 and 18

Girls from poorer households are more likely to become teenage mothers than are girls from wealthier households.

Had a child or is currently pregnant, most recent value in 2008–16 (% of women ages 15–19)

● Richest quintile ● Poorest quintile

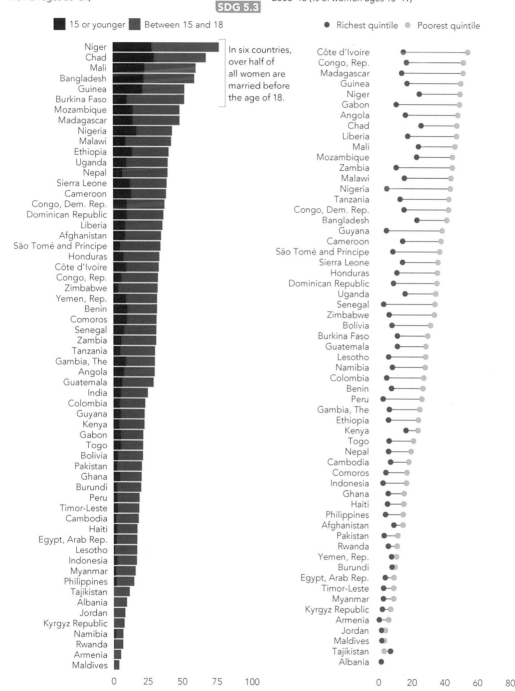

In six countries, over half of all women are married before the age of 18.

Source: Household surveys (DHS) and World Bank Women, Business and the Law. World Development Indicators (SP.M18.2024.FE.ZS; SP.M15.2024.FE.ZS).

Source: Household surveys (DHS, MICS). Health Nutrition and Population Statistics by Wealth Quintile (SP.MTR.1519.Q1.ZS; SP.MTR.1519.Q5.ZS).

Women lag behind men in business ownership. In every region, on average less than half of firms are even partially owned by women.

Firms with female participation in ownership, by country and regional median, most recent value in 2010–17 (%) `SDG 5.5`

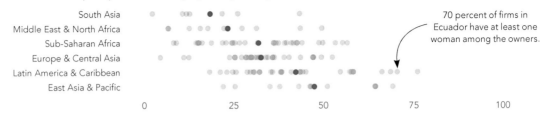

70 percent of firms in Ecuador have at least one woman among the owners.

Note: Aggregates are based mostly on low- and middle-income countries.
Source: World Bank Enterprise Surveys. World Development Indicators (IC.FRM.FEMO.ZS).

In political life, men are overrepresented. Across regions, women on average occupy less than a quarter of parliamentary seats.

Proportion of seats held by women in national parliaments, by country and regional median, 2017 (%) `SDG 5.5`

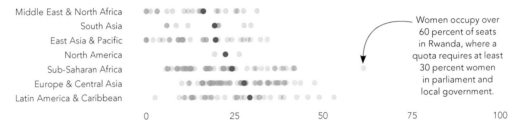

Women occupy over 60 percent of seats in Rwanda, where a quota requires at least 30 percent women in parliament and local government.

Source: Inter-Parliamentary Union. World Development Indicators (SG.GEN.PARL.ZS).

Women average 2.6 times as much time on unpaid care and domestic work as men do.

Proportion of time spent on unpaid care and domestic work, most recent value in 2007–15 (% of 24 hour day) `SDG 5.4`

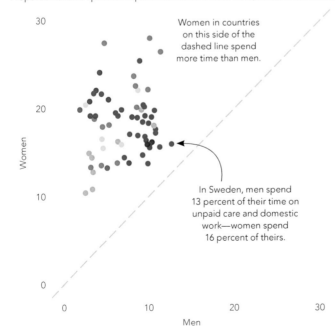

Women in countries on this side of the dashed line spend more time than men.

- East Asia & Pacific
- Europe & Central Asia
- Latin America & Caribbean
- Middle East & North Africa
- North America
- South Asia
- Sub-Saharan Africa

In Sweden, men spend 13 percent of their time on unpaid care and domestic work—women spend 16 percent of theirs.

Unpaid care and domestic work include chores such as cooking and cleaning and the care of family members such as children and the elderly. This work places a burden on women's time and can limit their ability to participate in the labor force.

Note: 2.6 times estimate from UN Women (2018) http://www.unwomen.org/en/digital-library/sdg-report. Data may not be strictly comparable across countries as the method and sampling used for data collection may differ.
Source: UN Statistics Division. World Development Indicators (SG.TIM.UWRK.MA, SG.TIM.UWRK.FE).

Many women in Sub-Saharan Africa are not free to make their own decisions about reproductive health and sexual relations.

Women making their own informed decisions regarding sexual relations, contraceptive use, and reproductive healthcare, most recent value in 2007–15 (% of women ages 15–49)

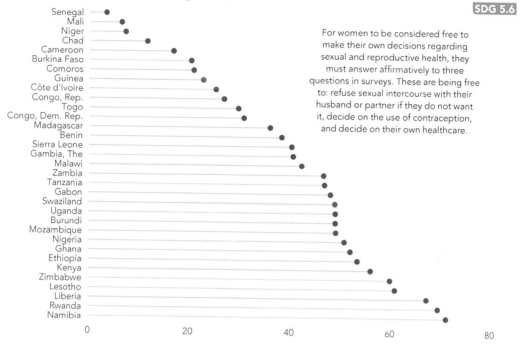

For women to be considered free to make their own decisions regarding sexual and reproductive health, they must answer affirmatively to three questions in surveys. These are being free to: refuse sexual intercourse with their husband or partner if they do not want it, decide on the use of contraception, and decide on their own healthcare.

Note: Countries in Sub-Saharan Africa with available data shown.
Source: Household surveys (DHS) compiled by United Nations Population Fund. WDI (SG.DMK.SRCR.FN.ZS).

Women with greater decision making power are more likely to use modern contraceptive methods and to have fewer children.

Most recent value in 2007–15

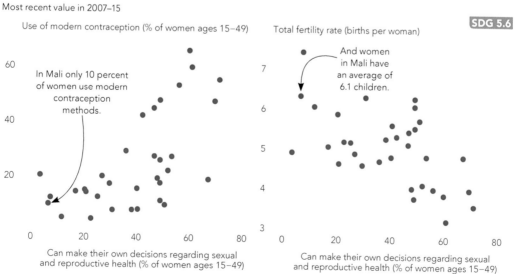

Note: All countries plotted are in Sub-Saharan Africa.
Source: Household surveys (DHS, MICS) and UN Population Division. WDI (SP.DYN.CONM.ZS; SG.DMK.SRCR.FN.ZS; SP.DYN.TFRT.IN).

Clean water and sanitation

Ensure availability and sustainable management of water and sanitation for all

Drinking water is essential to life, but only 71 percent of people have water that is considered safely managed.

Access to water at different categories, 2015 (% of global population)

`SDG 6.1`

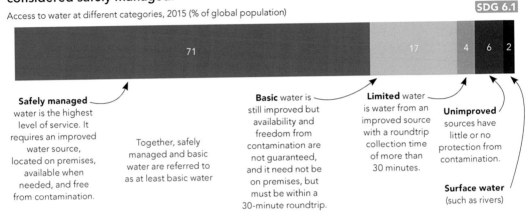

| 71 | 17 | 4 | 6 | 2 |

Safely managed water is the highest level of service. It requires an improved water source, located on premises, available when needed, and free from contamination.

Together, safely managed and basic water are referred to as at least basic water

Basic water is still improved but availability and freedom from contamination are not guaranteed, and it need not be on premises, but must be within a 30-minute roundtrip.

Limited water is water from an improved source with a roundtrip collection time of more than 30 minutes.

Unimproved sources have little or no protection from contamination.

Surface water (such as rivers)

Source: WHO/UNICEF JMP for Water Supply, Sanitation and Hygiene, https://washdata.org. WDI (SH.H2O.SMDW.ZS; SH.BASW.ZS).

Countries may have similar rates of safely managed access for different reasons.

Components of safely managed water for two countries, 2015 (% of population)

`SDG 6.1`

In both Ghana and Nepal an estimated 27 percent of people have access to safely managed water. However, the limiting factor in Ghana is accessibility, whereas in Nepal it is contamination.

— Safely managed

Accessible on premises
Available when needed
Free from contamination

Ghana   Nepal

Source: WHO/UNICEF Joint Monitoring Programme for Water Supply, Sanitation and Hygiene, https://washdata.org. WDI (SH.H2O.SMDW.ZS).

In Sub-Saharan Africa 58% of people have access to at least basic water, but less than half of those have access to safely managed water.

Access to safely managed and basic water, 2015 (% of population)

`SDG 6.1`

At least basic
Basic
Safely managed

Sub-Saharan Africa | Latin America & Caribbean | Middle East & North Africa | Europe & Central Asia | North America | South Asia[a] | East Asia & Pacific[a]

a. Too few countries have data on safely managed water to calculate the regional aggregate for South Asia and East Asia & Pacific.

Source: WHO/UNICEF JMP for Water Supply, Sanitation and Hygiene, https://washdata.org. WDI (SH.H2O.SMDW.ZS; SH.BASW.ZS).

At least basic water requires only an improved water source within a 30-minute roundtrip, but 42 percent of people in Sub-Saharan Africa lack even that.

People using at least basic water services, 2015 (% of population)

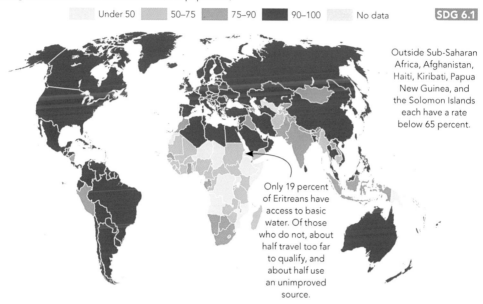

Under 50   50–75   75–90   90–100   No data   **SDG 6.1**

Outside Sub-Saharan Africa, Afghanistan, Haiti, Kiribati, Papua New Guinea, and the Solomon Islands each have a rate below 65 percent.

Only 19 percent of Eritreans have access to basic water. Of those who do not, about half travel too far to qualify, and about half use an unimproved source.

Source: WHO/UNICEF Joint Monitoring Programme for Water Supply, Sanitation and Hygiene. World Development Indicators (SH.H2O.BASW.ZS).

Rural dwellers are less likely than their urban counterparts to have access to at least basic water.

People using at least basic water services (%)

SDG 6.1

East Asia & Pacific
Urban
Rural
   2000   2015

Europe & Central Asia
Urban
Rural

Latin America & Caribbean
Urban
Rural

Middle East & North Africa
Urban
Rural

North America
Urban
Rural

South Asia
Urban
Rural

Sub–Saharan Africa
Urban
Rural

0   25   50   75   100

Note: Data not available for North America (rural) for 2000.
Source: WDI (SH.H2O.BASW.UR.ZS; SH.H2O.BASW.RU.ZS).

Poorer people are less likely to have the convenience and potential safety of water piped to their homes.

People using piped water on premises, most recent value (%)

SDG 6.1

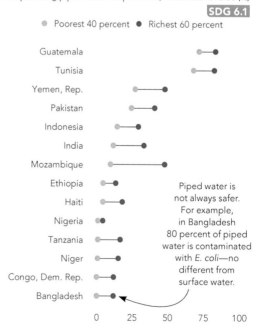

● Poorest 40 percent   ● Richest 60 percent

Guatemala
Tunisia
Yemen, Rep.
Pakistan
Indonesia
India
Mozambique
Ethiopia
Haiti
Nigeria
Tanzania
Niger
Congo, Dem. Rep.
Bangladesh

0   25   50   75   100

Piped water is not always safer. For example, in Bangladesh 80 percent of piped water is contaminated with E. coli—no different from surface water.

Source: World Bank (2017). http://hdl.handle.net/10986/27831

Globally, 6 in 10 people use sanitation facilities that are not safely managed and may contribute to the spread of disease.

Access to sanitation at different categories, 2015 (% of global population)

`SDG 6.2`

Safely managed sanitation requires use of improved facilities that are not shared with other households and where excreta are safely disposed of in situ or offsite.

Together, safely managed and basic sanitation are referred to as at least basic sanitation

Basic sanitation is the use of an improved facility that is not shared with other households

Limited sanitation means an improved facility that is shared among multiple households.

Unimproved sanitation facilities do not hygienically separate excreta from human contact.

Open defecation (such as fields and forests)

Source: WHO/UNICEF JMP for Water Supply, Sanitation and Hygiene, https://washdata.org. WDI (SH.STA.SMSS.ZS; SH.STA.BASS.ZS).

In Latin America & Caribbean 86 percent of people have access to at least basic sanitation, but only a quarter of those have access to safely managed sanitation.

Access to safely managed and basic sanitation, 2015 (% of population)

`SDG 6.2`

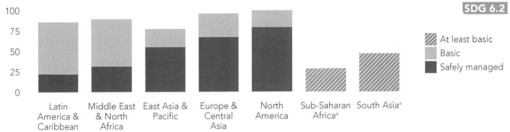

Legend:
- ▨ At least basic
- ▨ Basic
- ▨ Safely managed

a. Too few countries have data on safely managed sanitation to calculate the regional aggregate for Sub-Saharan Africa and South Asia.
Source: WHO/UNICEF Joint Monitoring Programme for Water Supply, Sanitation and Hygiene, WDI (SH.STA.SMSS.ZS; SH.STA.BASS.ZS).

Even by the less demanding standard of at least basic sanitation, many countries, especially in Sub-Saharan Africa, have very low rates of access.

Access to at least basic sanitation, 2015 (% of population)

`SDG 6.2`

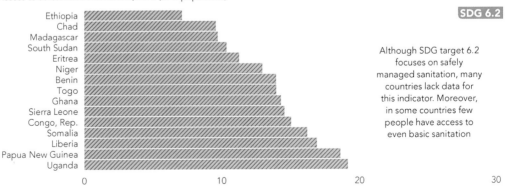

Although SDG target 6.2 focuses on safely managed sanitation, many countries lack data for this indicator. Moreover, in some countries few people have access to even basic sanitation

Note: The 15 countries with lowest access to at least basic sanitation (out of 210 countries with data).
Source: WHO/UNICEF Joint Monitoring Programme for Water Supply, Sanitation and Hygiene, World Development Indicators (SH.STA.BASS.ZS).

India still has the largest number of people practicing open defecation.

People practicing open defecation (millions)

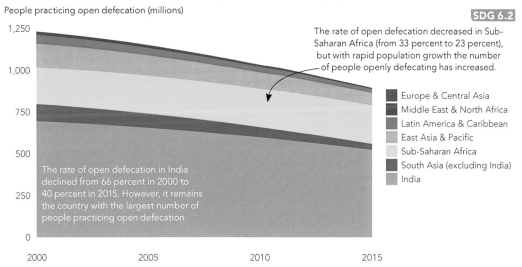

SDG 6.2

The rate of open defecation decreased in Sub-Saharan Africa (from 33 percent to 23 percent), but with rapid population growth the number of people openly defecating has increased.

Europe & Central Asia
Middle East & North Africa
Latin America & Caribbean
East Asia & Pacific
Sub-Saharan Africa
South Asia (excluding India)
India

The rate of open defecation in India declined from 66 percent in 2000 to 40 percent in 2015. However, it remains the country with the largest number of people practicing open defecation.

Note: North America is zero over the entire period; Europe & Central Asia is zero from 2013.
Source: WHO/UNICEF Joint Monitoring Programme for Water Supply, Sanitation and Hygiene. WDI (SH.STA.ODFC.ZS; SP.POP.TOTL).

Handwashing makes an important contribution to hygiene, but many households, especially among the poor, lack basic facilities.

Access to handwashing facilities with soap and water on premises, most recent value in 2010–14 (%)

SDG 6.2

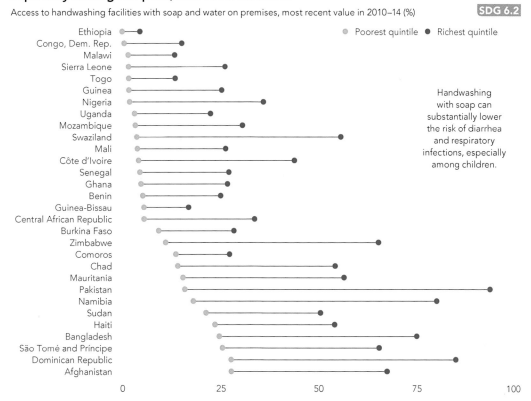

Handwashing with soap can substantially lower the risk of diarrhea and respiratory infections, especially among children.

Note: The 30 countries with lowest access among the poorest wealth quintile (out of 51 countries with data).
Source: WHO/UNICEF Joint Monitoring Programme for Water Supply, Sanitation and Hygiene. WDI (SH.STA.HYGN.Q1.ZS; SH.STA.HYGN.Q5.ZS).

Affordable and clean energy

Ensure access to affordable, reliable, sustainable and modern energy for all

Population growth has outpaced energy infrastructure development in Sub-Saharan Africa, where more people now live without electricity than in 1990.

People without access to electricity, 1990 and 2016

- East Asia & Pacific
- Europe & Central Asia
- Latin America & Caribbean
- Middle East & North Africa
- South Asia
- Sub-Saharan Africa

SDG 7.1

1990

India 493 million

Bangladesh | Pakistan | Nepal | Afghanistan | Sri Lanka

Nigeria | Ethiopia | Congo, Dem. Rep. | Tanzania | Uganda

Sudan | Kenya | Mozambique | Madagascar | Burkina Faso | South Africa | Chad | Niger | Zambia | Mali | Ghana | South Sudan | Somalia | Cameroon | Guinea | Benin | Angola | Zimbabwe | Côte d'Ivoire | Sierraz Leone | Senegal | Malawi | Burundi | Rwanda

China | Indonesia | Philippines | Korea, Dem. People's Rep. | Brazil | Haiti | Vietnam | Cambodia | Peru | Myanmar | Thailand | Papua New Guinea | Morocco | Yemen, Rep. | Turkey

India has increased access to electricity from 43 percent to 84 percent of the population, but many remain without, especially in rural areas.

In East Asia & Pacific several countries, including China and Thailand, attained universal access (SDG target 7.1) between 1990 and 2016.

In Sub-Saharan Africa only a few countries have substantially reduced the number of people without access, most notably South Africa and Ghana.

2016

India 205 million

Bangladesh | Pakistan | Nepal | Afghanistan | Sri Lanka

Nigeria | Ethiopia | Congo, Dem. Rep. | Tanzania | Uganda

Sudan | Kenya | Mozambique | Madagascar | Burkina Faso | South Africa | Chad | Niger | Zambia | Mali | Ghana | South Sudan | Somalia | Cameroon | Guinea | Benin | Angola | Zimbabwe | Côte d'Ivoire | Sierra Leone | Senegal | Malawi | Burundi | Rwanda

China | Indonesia | Philippines | Korea, Dem. People's Rep. | Brazil | Haiti | Vietnam | Cambodia | Peru | Myanmar | Thailand | Papua New Guinea | Morocco | Yemen, Rep. | Turkey

Source: World Bank, World Development Indicators (EG.ELC.ACCS.ZS; SP.POP.TOTL).

Worldwide, 3 billion people lack access to clean cooking fuels and instead use fuels that create health risks.

People without access to clean fuels and technologies for cooking, 2016

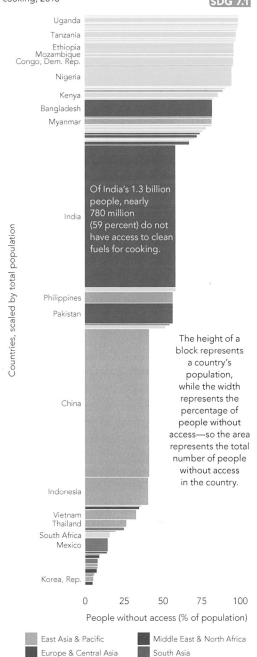

Of India's 1.3 billion people, nearly 780 million (59 percent) do not have access to clean fuels for cooking.

The height of a block represents a country's population, while the width represents the percentage of people without access—so the area represents the total number of people without access in the country.

People without access (% of population)

Legend:
- East Asia & Pacific
- Europe & Central Asia
- Latin America & Caribbean
- Middle East & North Africa
- South Asia
- Sub-Saharan Africa

Note: Excludes countries with a population of less than 10 million or an access rate above 95 percent.

Source: WHO. WDI (EG.CFT.ACCS.ZS; SP.POP.TOTL).

In South Asia and Sub-Saharan Africa gains in access to clean fuels have not kept up with those in access to electricity

Access rates, 2000 and 2016 (% of population)

● 2000 ▶ 2016

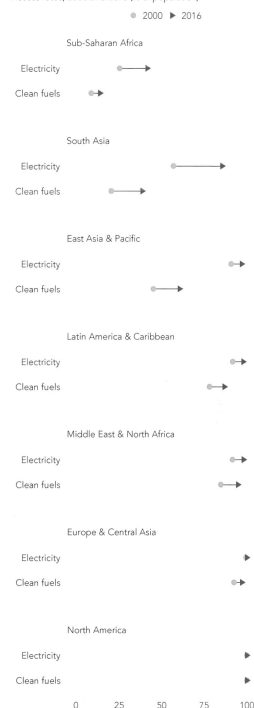

Source: World Bank, WHO. WDI (EG.ELC.ACCS.ZS; EG.CFT.ACCS.ZS).

Renewable energy accounts for a large share of energy consumption in Sub-Saharan Africa, but that often reflects burning of biomass in traditional ways in open fires.

Renewable energy consumption, 2015 (% of total final energy consumption)

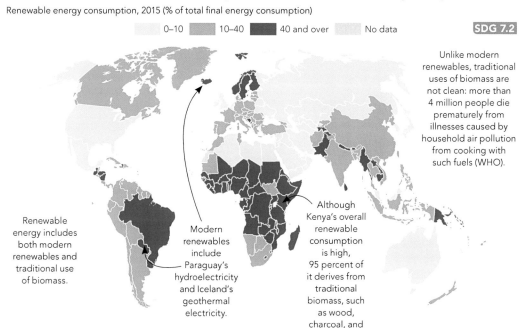

0–10 ■ 10–40 ■ 40 and over ⬚ No data — SDG 7.2

Unlike modern renewables, traditional uses of biomass are not clean: more than 4 million people die prematurely from illnesses caused by household air pollution from cooking with such fuels (WHO).

Renewable energy includes both modern renewables and traditional use of biomass.

Modern renewables include Paraguay's hydroelectricity and Iceland's geothermal electricity.

Although Kenya's overall renewable consumption is high, 95 percent of it derives from traditional biomass, such as wood, charcoal, and animal waste.

Source: IEA, UNSD. World Development Indicators (EG.FEC.RNEW.ZS).

Modern renewables still make a modest contribution across all income groups.

Global total final energy consumption, by income group and source, 2015 (% of income group total)

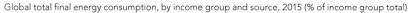

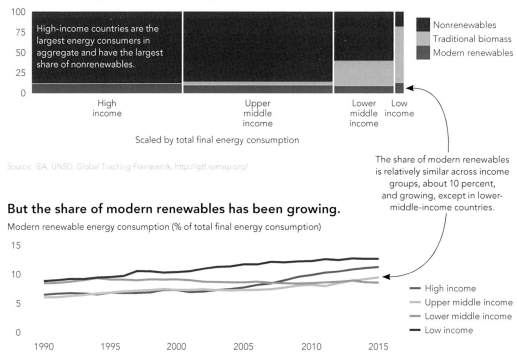

High-income countries are the largest energy consumers in aggregate and have the largest share of nonrenewables.

Nonrenewables
Traditional biomass
Modern renewables

High income   Upper middle income   Lower middle income   Low income

Scaled by total final energy consumption

Source: IEA, UNSD. Global Tracking Framework. http://gtf.esmap.org/

The share of modern renewables is relatively similar across income groups, about 10 percent, and growing, except in lower-middle-income countries.

But the share of modern renewables has been growing.

Modern renewable energy consumption (% of total final energy consumption)

High income
Upper middle income
Lower middle income
Low income

Source: IEA, UNSD. Global Tracking Framework. http://gtf.esmap.org/

The amount of energy used to produce one dollar's worth of goods and services varies around the world.

Energy intensity of primary energy, 2015 (MJ/2011 PPP$ GDP)

0–5   5–10   10 and over   No data   SDG 7.3

For reference, one liter of petrol (gasoline) produces about 33 MJ (megajoules) of energy.

A country's energy intensity reflects both the mix of industries it hosts and the energy efficiency of those industries.

Source: IEA, UNSD, and World Bank. World Development Indicators (EG.EGY.PRIM.PP.KD).

Energy intensity has fallen everywhere but the Middle East & North Africa.

Energy intensity of primary energy (MJ/2011 PPP$ GDP)

◀ 2015   ● 1990

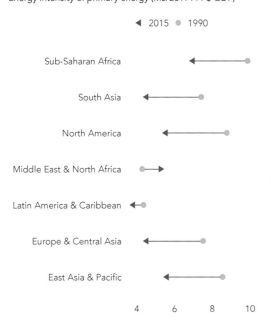

- Sub-Saharan Africa
- South Asia
- North America
- Middle East & North Africa
- Latin America & Caribbean
- Europe & Central Asia
- East Asia & Pacific

4   6   8   10

Source: IEA, UNSD, and World Bank. WDI (EG.EGY.PRIM.PP.KD).

And globally, energy intensity has fallen in all sectors.

Energy intensity (MJ/2011 PPP$ GDP)

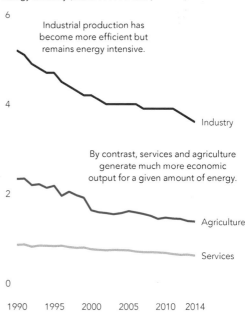

Industrial production has become more efficient but remains energy intensive.

Industry

By contrast, services and agriculture generate much more economic output for a given amount of energy.

Agriculture

Services

1990   1995   2000   2005   2010   2014

Source: IEA, UNSD, and World Bank. http://gtf.esmap.org/

Decent work and economic growth

Promote sustained, inclusive and sustainable economic growth, full and productive employment and decent work for all

Many Least Developed Countries have seen economic growth in the last decade, but few have achieved the SDG target of 7 percent a year.

Average annual GDP and GDP per capita growth, 2007–16 (%)

SDG 8.1

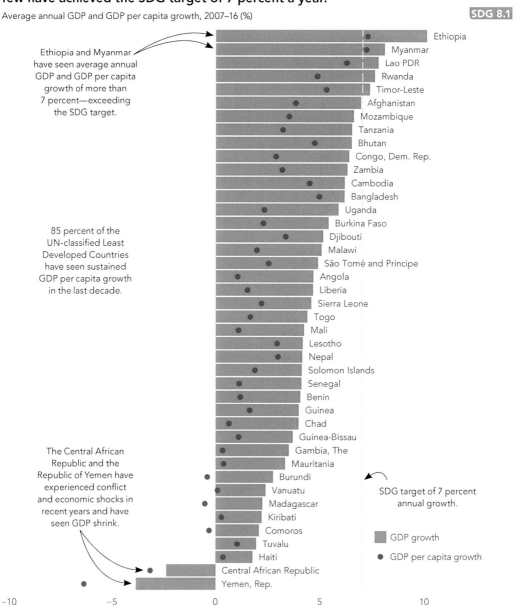

Ethiopia and Myanmar have seen average annual GDP and GDP per capita growth of more than 7 percent—exceeding the SDG target.

85 percent of the UN-classified Least Developed Countries have seen sustained GDP per capita growth in the last decade.

The Central African Republic and the Republic of Yemen have experienced conflict and economic shocks in recent years and have seen GDP shrink.

SDG target of 7 percent annual growth.

Ethiopia
Myanmar
Lao PDR
Rwanda
Timor-Leste
Afghanistan
Mozambique
Tanzania
Bhutan
Congo, Dem. Rep.
Zambia
Cambodia
Bangladesh
Uganda
Burkina Faso
Djibouti
Malawi
São Tomé and Príncipe
Angola
Liberia
Sierra Leone
Togo
Mali
Lesotho
Nepal
Solomon Islands
Senegal
Benin
Guinea
Chad
Guinea-Bissau
Gambia, The
Mauritania
Burundi
Vanuatu
Madagascar
Kiribati
Comoros
Tuvalu
Haiti
Central African Republic
Yemen, Rep.

GDP growth
● GDP per capita growth

−10   −5   0   5   10

Note: Data are not available for Djibouti, Eritrea, Niger, Somalia, South Sudan, and Sudan.
Source: World Bank national accounts data and OECD National Accounts data files. WDI (NY.GDP.MKTP.KD; NY.GDP.PCAP.KD).

Agriculture dominates employment in South Asia and Sub-Saharan Africa, while most people in Europe & Central Asia, Latin America & Caribbean, and North America work in the service sector.

Employment by sector, 2016 (% of total employment)

SDG 8.2
SDG 8.3

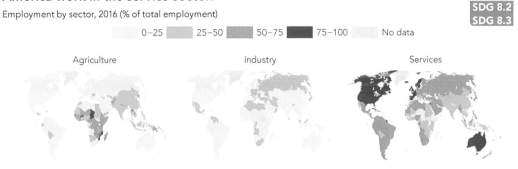

0–25   25–50   50–75   75–100   No data

Agriculture   Industry   Services

Source: ILO. World Development Indicators (SL.AGR.EMPL.ZS; SL.IND.EMPL.ZS; SL.SRV.EMPL.ZS).

In the early 2000s the service sector overtook agriculture to become the world's largest employer. Globally, services account for 50 percent of employment, agriculture 30 percent, and industry 20 percent.

Employment by sector (% of total employment)

SDG 8.2
SDG 8.3

Agriculture   Industry   Services

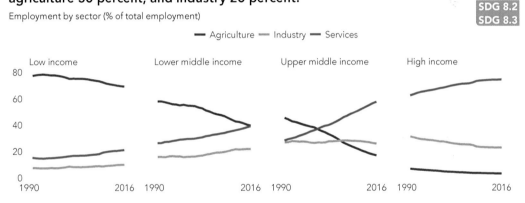

Source: ILO. World Development Indicators (SL.AGR.EMPL.ZS; SL.IND.EMPL.ZS; SL.SRV.EMPL.ZS).

Not everyone of working age can find employment, especially young people. And as populations age, the share of the population that is working falls.

People (billions)

SDG 8.5

Employed ages 15 and older   Population ages 15 and older

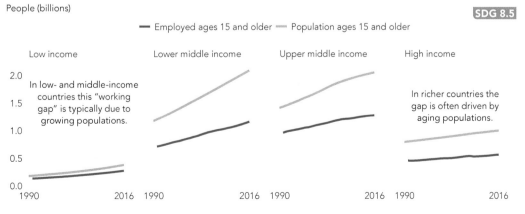

Source: ILO. WDI (SP.POP.TOTL; SP.POP.1564.TO.ZS; SP.POP.65UP.TO.ZS; SL.EMP.TOTL.SP.ZS).

Globally, women are less likely to be employed than men, but the gap is most pronounced in lower-middle-income countries.

Share of people by employment status, 2016 (% of population ages 15 and older)

SDG 8.5

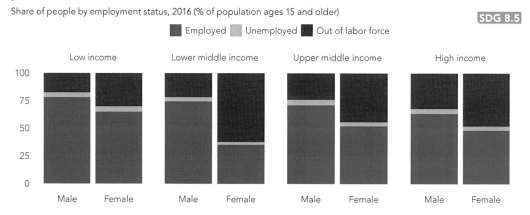

Source: ILO. World Development Indicators (SL.UEM.TOTL.FE.ZS; SL.UEM.TOTL.MA.ZS; SL.TLF.CACT.FE.ZS; SL.TLF.CACT.MA.ZS; SL.EMP.TOTL.SP.FE.ZS; SL.EMP.TOTL.SP.MA.ZS; SP.POP.1564.FE.ZS; SP.POP.65UP.FE.ZS; SP.POP.1564.MA.ZS; SP.POP.65UP.MA.ZS).

Many people in South Asia and Sub-Saharan Africa work for themselves or their family. They are more likely to lack social safety nets, and they face a greater risk from economic shocks than salaried workers do.

Employment type, 2016 (% of total employment)

SDG 8.3

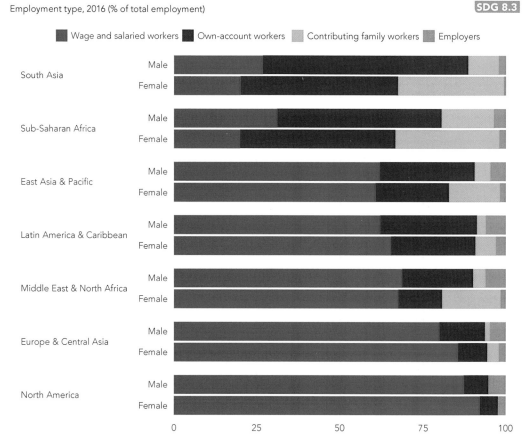

Source: ILO. World Development Indicators (SL.EMP.MPYR.FE.ZS; SL.EMP.MPYR.MA.ZS; SL.EMP.WORK.FE.ZS; SL.EMP.WORK.MA.ZS; SL.EMP.OWAC.FE.ZS; SL.EMP.OWAC.MA.ZS; SL.FAM.WORK.FE.ZS; SL.FAM.WORK.MA.ZS).

Access to financial services benefits individuals and societies. Globally, 69 percent of adults have an account with a financial institution or mobile money provider.

Account ownership, 2017 (% of population ages 15 and older)

SDG 8.10

Legend: 0–20 | 20–40 | 40–65 | 65–90 | 90–100 | No data

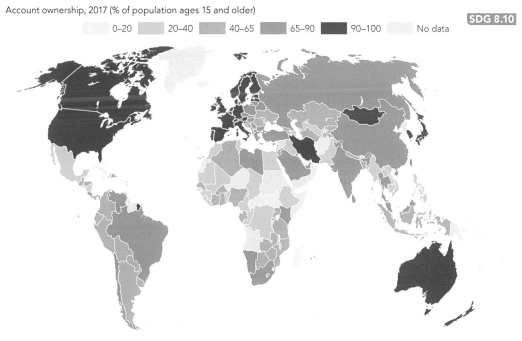

Source: Global Findex Database, World Development Indicators (FX.OWN.TOTL.ZS).

Financial account ownership is lower among younger adults, those with less education, women, and poorer adults.

Account ownership, 2017 (% of population ages 15 and older)

SDG 8.10

- Ages 25 and older
- Ages 15–24
- Secondary or more
- Primary or less
- Male
- Female
- Richest 60 percent
- Poorest 40 percent

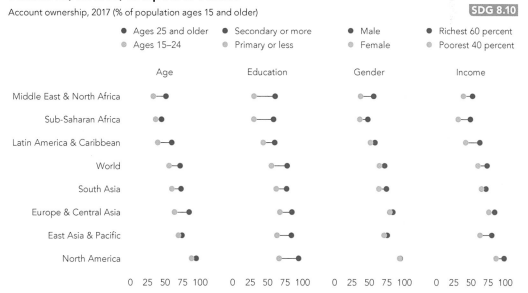

Note: Data refer to the richest 60 percent and poorest 40 percent within individual economies rather than the region as a whole.

Source: Global Findex Database, World Development Indicators (FX.OWN.TOTL.MA.ZS; FX.OWN.TOTL.FE.ZS; FX.OWN.TOTL.YG.ZS; FX.OWN.TOTL.OL.ZS; FX.OWN.TOTL.PL.ZS; FX.OWN.TOTL.SO.ZS; FX.OWN.TOTL.40.ZS; FX.OWN.TOTL.60.ZS).

Industry, innovation, and infrastructure

Build resilient infrastructure, promote inclusive and sustainable industrialization and foster innovation

Infrastructure supports communities. Without access to an all-season road, people are cut off from crucial services and markets.

Access to an all-season road, within 2 km, most recent value in 2009–16

People with access (% of rural population)

People without access (millions)

Bangladesh
Kenya
Rwanda
Nepal
Uganda
Tanzania
Ethiopia
Mozambique
Lesotho
Zambia

This indicator is also known as the Rural Access Index (RAI).

Note: Data available for only 10 countries.
Source: World Bank 2016. http://hdl.handle.net/10986/25187

Access to physical infrastructure varies within countries: in Rwanda people living in rural areas in the east are less connected.

People within 2 km of an all-season road, Rwanda, by district, 2015 (% of rural population)

25–50   50–75   75–100

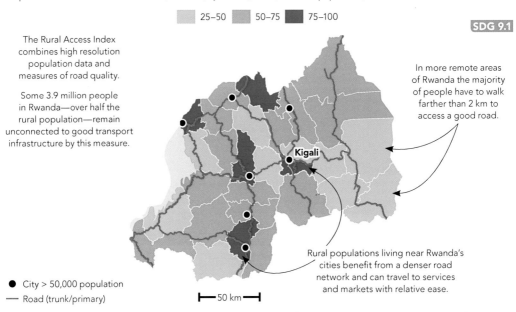

The Rural Access Index combines high resolution population data and measures of road quality.

Some 3.9 million people in Rwanda—over half the rural population—remain unconnected to good transport infrastructure by this measure.

In more remote areas of Rwanda the majority of people have to walk farther than 2 km to access a good road.

Kigali

Rural populations living near Rwanda's cities benefit from a denser road network and can travel to services and markets with relative ease.

● City > 50,000 population
— Road (trunk/primary)

⊢—50 km—⊣

Source: World Bank 2017. Rwanda - Feeder Roads Development Project: additional financing; Natural Earth; OpenStreetMap contributors.

The rural poor are often most affected by lack of access to good roads. In Kenya and Mozambique poverty and lack of access are closely correlated.

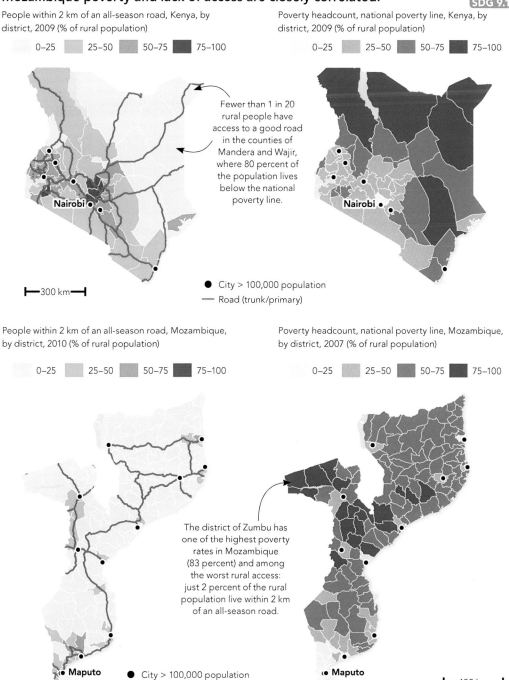

People within 2 km of an all-season road, Kenya, by district, 2009 (% of rural population)

0–25   25–50   50–75   75–100

Poverty headcount, national poverty line, Kenya, by district, 2009 (% of rural population)

0–25   25–50   50–75   75–100

Nairobi

Fewer than 1 in 20 rural people have access to a good road in the counties of Mandera and Wajir, where 80 percent of the population lives below the national poverty line.

Nairobi

300 km

● City > 100,000 population
— Road (trunk/primary)

People within 2 km of an all-season road, Mozambique, by district, 2010 (% of rural population)

0–25   25–50   50–75   75–100

Poverty headcount, national poverty line, Mozambique, by district, 2007 (% of rural population)

0–25   25–50   50–75   75–100

The district of Zumbu has one of the highest poverty rates in Mozambique (83 percent) and among the worst rural access: just 2 percent of the rural population live within 2 km of an all-season road.

● Maputo

● Maputo

● City > 100,000 population
— Road (trunk/primary)

400 km

Source: World Bank 2017, http://hdl.handle.net/10986/25187; Natural Earth; OpenStreetMap contributors.

Manufacturing and other industry is a large source of employment. But many Least Developed Countries have a small manufacturing sector.

GDP per capita, by sector value added, 2000–16 (constant 2010 US$, each country scaled independently)

SDG 9.2

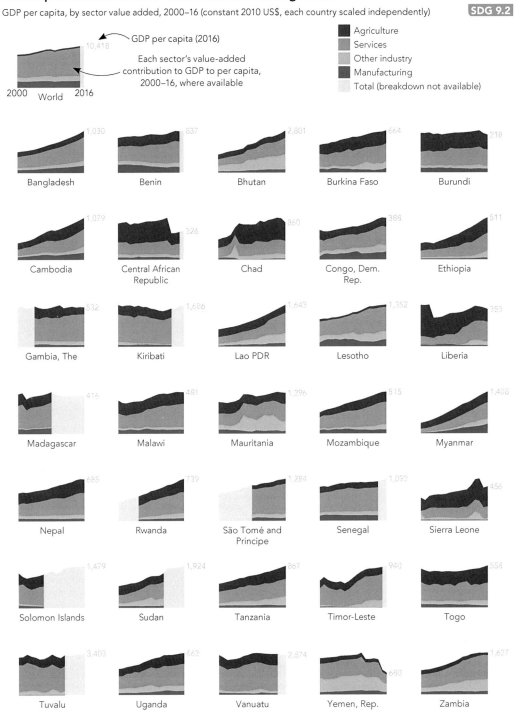

GDP per capita (2016)

Each sector's value-added contribution to GDP to per capita, 2000–16, where available

2000   World   2016

- Agriculture
- Services
- Other industry
- Manufacturing
- Total (breakdown not available)

Bangladesh 1,030	Benin 837	Bhutan 2,601	Burkina Faso 664	Burundi 218
Cambodia 1,079	Central African Republic 326	Chad 860	Congo, Dem. Rep. 388	Ethiopia 511
Gambia, The 532	Kiribati 1,686	Lao PDR 1,643	Lesotho 1,352	Liberia 353
Madagascar 416	Malawi 481	Mauritania 1,296	Mozambique 515	Myanmar 1,408
Nepal 685	Rwanda 739	São Tomé and Príncipe 1,284	Senegal 1,092	Sierra Leone 456
Solomon Islands 1,479	Sudan 1,924	Tanzania 867	Timor-Leste 940	Togo 558
Tuvalu 3,403	Uganda 662	Vanuatu 2,874	Yemen, Rep. 680	Zambia 1,627

Note: Includes Least Developed Countries (UN classification) with complete GDP per capita data and at least five years of sector value-added data.
Source: World Bank and OECD. WDI (NV.IND.MANF.ZS; NV.IND.TOTL.ZS; NV.AGR.TOTL.ZS; NV.SRV.TETC.ZS; NY.GDP.PCAP.KD).

Medium- and high-tech industry allows for greater diversification and offers better opportunities for skills development and innovation.

Medium- and high-tech industry (% manufacturing value added)

0–15   15–30   30 and over   No data   SDG 9.b

Medium- and high-tech industries include the manufacture of chemicals, machinery, and motor vehicles.

Source: UNIDO. World Development Indicators (NV.MNF.TECH.ZS.UN).

Patents are designed to encourage innovation by providing incentives for research and development.

Patent applications, residents, top six countries in 2016

SDG 9.5

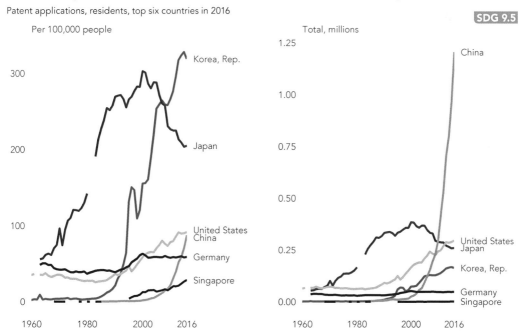

Source: WIPO. World Development Indicators (IP.PAT.RESD; SP.POP.TOTL).

Reduced inequalities

Reduce inequality within and among countries

There is great inequality across countries and regions. North America is 3.5 times richer than the world average, but its relative income per capita has been falling. By contrast, relative incomes are rising in South Asia and East Asia & Pacific.

Relative GDP per capita (1x = world average)

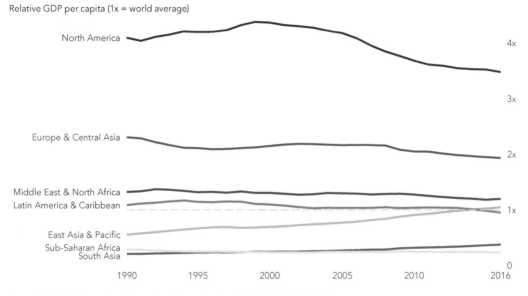

Source: World Bank, International Comparison Program database. WDI (NY.GDP.PCAP.PP.KD).

One simple way to measure inequality within a country is to consider the share of people living below 50 percent of its median income.

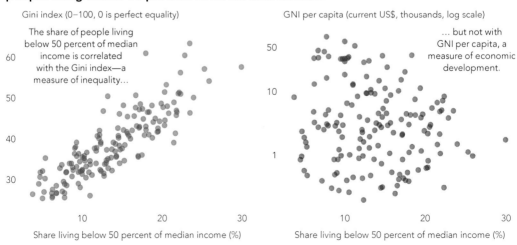

Gini index (0–100, 0 is perfect equality)

The share of people living below 50 percent of median income is correlated with the Gini index—a measure of inequality...

GNI per capita (current US$, thousands, log scale)

... but not with GNI per capita, a measure of economic development.

Share living below 50 percent of median income (%)

Source: World Bank PovcalNet (database). WDI (SI.POV.GINI; NY.GNP.PCAP.CD).

Changes in inequality can be measured by the relative income growth of the poorest 40 percent of people.

Annualized growth rate, Peru, 2009–14 (%)

`SDG 10.1`

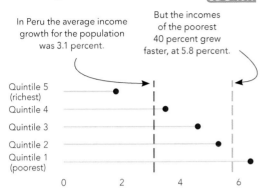

In Peru the average income growth for the population was 3.1 percent.

But the incomes of the poorest 40 percent grew faster, at 5.8 percent.

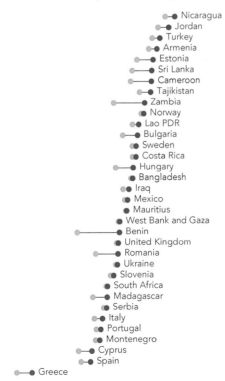

Source: World Bank Global Database of Shared Prosperity. WDI (SP.SPR.PCAP.ZG; SP.SPR.PC40.ZG; SI.SPR.PCAP; SI.DST.FRST.20; SI.DST.02ND.20; SI.DST.03RD.20; SI.DST.04TH.20; SI.DST.05TH.20).

In 34 countries income growth among the poorest was slower than average.

Annualized growth rate, circa 2009–14 (%)

`SDG 10.1`

● Poorest 40 percent   ● Average

Nicaragua
Jordan
Turkey
Armenia
Estonia
Sri Lanka
Cameroon
Tajikistan
Zambia
Norway
Lao PDR
Bulgaria
Sweden
Costa Rica
Hungary
Bangladesh
Iraq
Mexico
Mauritius
West Bank and Gaza
Benin
United Kingdom
Romania
Ukraine
Slovenia
South Africa
Madagascar
Serbia
Italy
Portugal
Montenegro
Cyprus
Spain
Greece

−10   −5   0   5

Note: Growth rates refer to real survey mean consumption or income.
Source: World Bank Global Database of Shared Prosperity. WDI (SI.SPR.PC40.ZG; SI.SPR.PCAP.ZG).

In 61 countries income growth among the poorest was faster than average.

Annualized growth rate, circa 2009–14 (%)

`SDG 10.1`

● Poorest 40 percent   ● Average

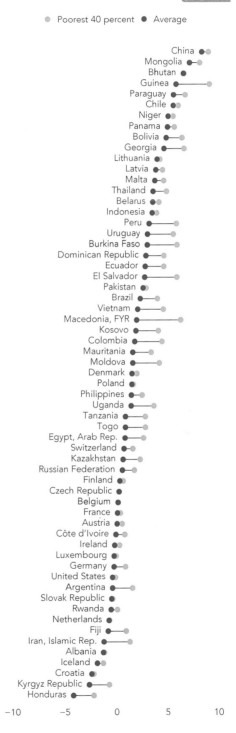

China
Mongolia
Bhutan
Guinea
Paraguay
Chile
Niger
Panama
Bolivia
Georgia
Lithuania
Latvia
Malta
Thailand
Belarus
Indonesia
Peru
Uruguay
Burkina Faso
Dominican Republic
Ecuador
El Salvador
Pakistan
Brazil
Vietnam
Macedonia, FYR
Kosovo
Colombia
Mauritania
Moldova
Denmark
Poland
Philippines
Uganda
Tanzania
Togo
Egypt, Arab Rep.
Switzerland
Kazakhstan
Russian Federation
Finland
Czech Republic
Belgium
France
Austria
Côte d'Ivoire
Ireland
Luxembourg
Germany
United States
Argentina
Slovak Republic
Rwanda
Netherlands
Fiji
Iran, Islamic Rep.
Albania
Iceland
Croatia
Kyrgyz Republic
Honduras

−10   −5   0   5   10

Note: Growth rates refer to real survey mean consumption or income.
Source: World Bank Global Database of Shared Prosperity. WDI (SI.SPR.PC40.ZG; SI.SPR.PCAP.ZG).

Personal remittances are an important source of income for people in low- and middle-income countries. But the average cost of sending this money remains high.

Average cost of sending remittances to a country, Q1 2017 (% of transaction)

0–3   3–5   5–10   10 and above   No data   SDG 10.c

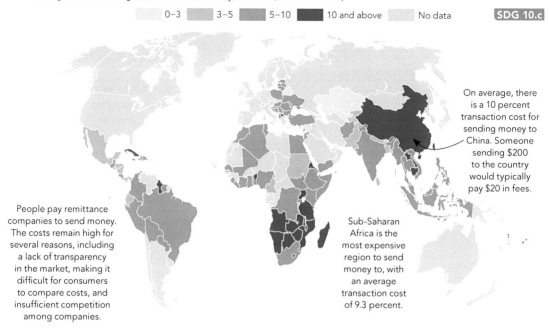

On average, there is a 10 percent transaction cost for sending money to China. Someone sending $200 to the country would typically pay $20 in fees.

People pay remittance companies to send money. The costs remain high for several reasons, including a lack of transparency in the market, making it difficult for consumers to compare costs, and insufficient competition among companies.

Sub-Saharan Africa is the most expensive region to send money to, with an average transaction cost of 9.3 percent.

Source: World Bank, Remittances Prices Worldwide (database) https://remittanceprices.worldbank.org/

The cost of sending remittances also varies by the country from which they are sent.

Average cost of sending remittances from a country, Q1 2017 (% of transaction)

0–3   3–5   5–10   10 and above   No data   SDG 10.c

It is cheap to send money from the Russian Federation, with an average transaction cost of 1.7 percent, and from India where the cost is under 1 percent.

The United States is the largest source of remittances in the world. Over $66 billion was sent in 2016. The average transaction cost to send those funds was 5.8 percent.

Source: World Bank, Remittances Prices Worldwide (database) https://remittanceprices.worldbank.org/

Globally, the average cost to send remittances fell from 9.1 percent to 7.1 percent over the last four years, but it remains above the SDG target of 3 percent.

Average cost of remittance services, by receiving region (% of transaction)

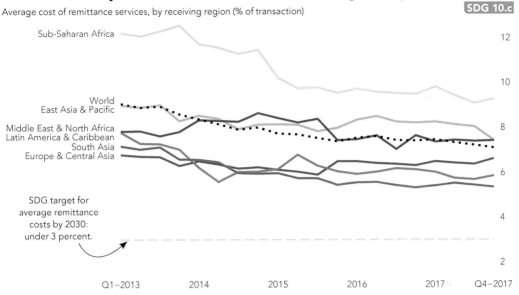

Source: Remittance Prices Worldwide, World Bank, Issue 24, https://remittanceprices.worldbank.org/

Remittance costs vary between sending and receiving country corridors. The SDG target aims to bring all corridor costs to below 5 percent of the amount remitted.

Average cost of sending remittances between countries (% of transaction)

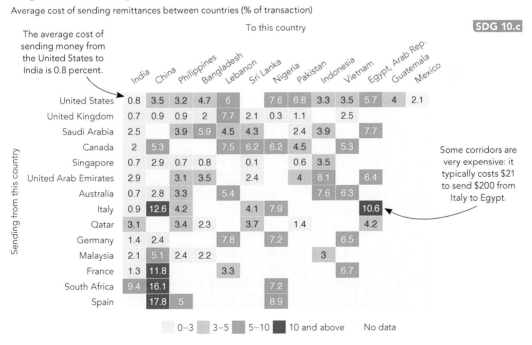

Note: The costs shown use the Smart Remitter Target methodology, which averages the three cheapest services for remitting money. Remittance corridors with the largest flows of money are shown. The dataset does not cover corridors where remittance flows are relatively small.

Source: World Bank, Remittances Prices Worldwide (database) https://remittanceprices.worldbank.org/

Sustainable cities and communities

Make cities and human settlements inclusive, safe, resilient and sustainable

Since about 2008 the majority of the world's population has lived in urban areas. Only South Asia and Sub-Saharan Africa remain more rural than urban.

Share of total population (%)

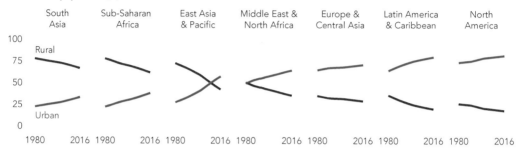

Source: UN Population Division, WDI (SP.URB.TOTL.IN.ZS; SP.RUR.TOTL.ZS).

Despite increasing urbanization, many countries have reduced the share of urban dwellers living in slums.

Population living in slums, 2005 and 2014 (% of urban population)

● 2005 ▶ 2014   `SDG 11.1`

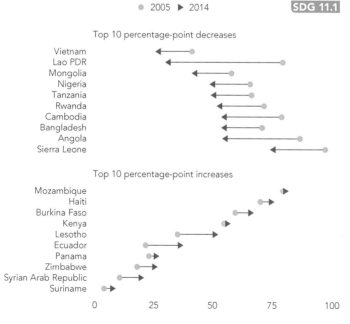

Source: UN-Habitat, World Development Indicators (EN.POP.SLUM.UR.ZS).

But substantial slum populations still exist.

Population, by locale, 2014 (%)

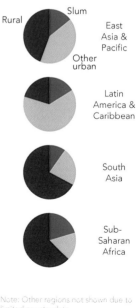

Note: Other regions not shown due to limited country data.

Source: WDI (EN.POP.SLUM.UR.ZS; SP.URB.TOTL.IN.ZS; SP.RUR.TOTL.ZS).

Reliable infrastructure helps cities to thrive: urban dwellers have better access to services and tend to be less poor than their rural counterparts.

Poverty headcount ratio at national poverty lines; and access to electricity, at least basic water and at least basic sanitation, countries with all four indicators available, 2014 (% of rural and urban populations)

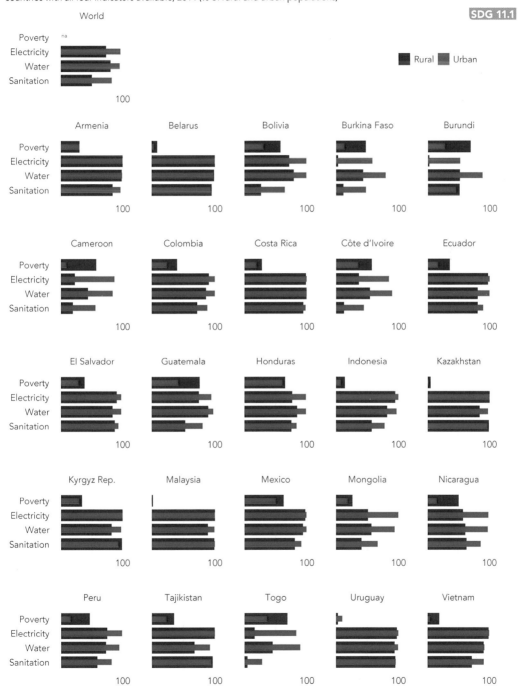

a. Poverty aggregate based on national poverty lines not available for world since these lines differ by country.

Source: World Bank; WHO; and WHO/UNICEF JMP for Water Supply, Sanitation and Hygiene. WDI (SI.POV.URHC; SI.POV.RUHC; EG.ELC.ACCS.UR.ZS; EG.ELC.ACCS.RU.ZS; SH.H2O.BASW.UR.ZS; SH.H2O.BASW.RU.ZS; SH.STA.BASS.UR.ZS; SH.STA.BASS.RU.ZS).

Atlas of Sustainable Development Goals 2018   43

Most countries exceed safe levels of fine particulate matter (PM$_{2.5}$) pollution. Industry, transport, and household uses of solid fuels are among the sources.

Ambient air pollution, PM$_{2.5}$, annual mean exposure, 2016 (micrograms per cubic meter, µg/m³)

SDG 11.6

- 0–10
- 10–25
- 25–35
- 35 and over
- No data

PM$_{2.5}$ particles are less than 2.5 microns in diameter and can penetrate deep into the respiratory tract.

WHO recommends that annual mean exposure to PM$_{2.5}$ pollution not exceed 10 micrograms per cubic meter.

PM$_{2.5}$ also comes from natural sources, for example windblown sand and dust in the Middle East and North Africa.

Mean exposure is based on population-weighted satellite measurements, calibrated to ground stations.

Source: van Donkelaar and others 2016. World Development Indicators (EN.ATM.PM25.MC.M3).

But PM$_{2.5}$ measurements show local variation from the national means.

PM$_{2.5}$, gridded by 0.1 degree, 2016 (µg/m³)

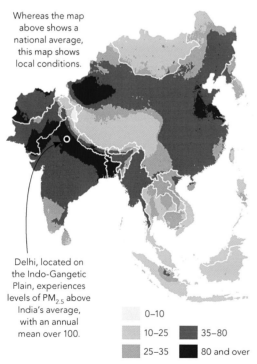

Whereas the map above shows a national average, this map shows local conditions.

Delhi, located on the Indo-Gangetic Plain, experiences levels of PM$_{2.5}$ above India's average, with an annual mean over 100.

- 0–10
- 10–25
- 25–35
- 35–80
- 80 and over

Source: van Donkelaar and others 2016. http://doi.org/10.1021/acs.est.5b05833

And even in a specific location, PM$_{2.5}$ varies with seasons and weather.

PM$_{2.5}$, daily mean, DTU[a] Delhi, 2017 (µg/m³)

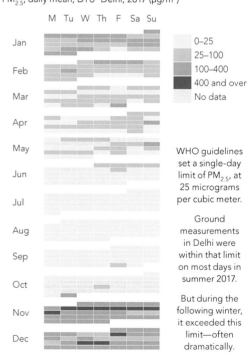

- 0–25
- 25–100
- 100–400
- 400 and over
- No data

WHO guidelines set a single-day limit of PM$_{2.5}$, at 25 micrograms per cubic meter.

Ground measurements in Delhi were within that limit on most days in summer 2017.

But during the following winter, it exceeded this limit—often dramatically.

a. Sampled at Delhi Technological University (DTU).

Source: India Central Pollution Control Board. https://app.cpcbccr.com

Ambient air pollution has many adverse consequences, including increased risk of premature death.

Deaths attributable to ambient air pollution, 2012 (per 100,000)

0–20 20–40 40 and over No data **SDG 11.6**

Air pollution disproportionately affects the elderly, so deaths attributable to it are especially high in countries with aging populations, such as the Russian Federation.

Household (indoor) pollution is also a serious problem, which can be reduced by adopting clean cooking fuels (SDG 7.1, see p. 27)

Source: WHO Global Health Observatory (database). http://apps.who.int/gho/data/view.main.BODAMBIENTAIRDTHS

In addition to the human toll, premature deaths attributable to air pollution have an economic cost to countries.

Estimated annual labor income losses from deaths due to air pollution, by type, 2015 (% of GDP)

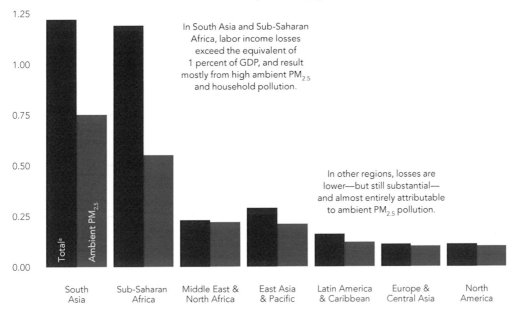

In South Asia and Sub-Saharan Africa, labor income losses exceed the equivalent of 1 percent of GDP, and result mostly from high ambient $PM_{2.5}$ and household pollution.

In other regions, losses are lower—but still substantial—and almost entirely attributable to ambient $PM_{2.5}$ pollution.

a. Includes losses attributable to household $PM_{2.5}$ air pollution and ambient ozone.

Source: World Bank 2016. http://hdl.handle.net/10986/29001

Responsible consumption and production

Ensure sustainable consumption and production patterns

People in high-income countries consume more extracted materials than people elsewhere do.

Material footprint, 2010 (metric tons per capita)

0–5　　5–10　　10–25　　25 and over　　No data

SDG 12.2

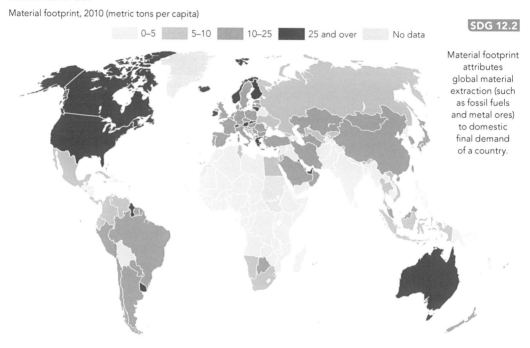

Material footprint attributes global material extraction (such as fossil fuels and metal ores) to domestic final demand of a country.

Source: UNEP (database). https://unstats.un.org/sdgs/indicators/database?indicator=12.2.1

China's material footprint increased threefold between 2000 and 2010, overtaking that of the United States in 2003.

Total material footprint (metric tons, billions)

SDG 12.2

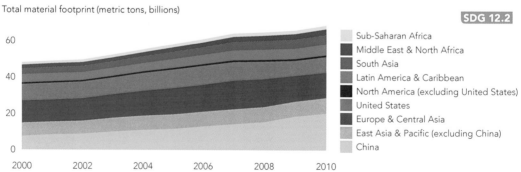

Sub-Saharan Africa
Middle East & North Africa
South Asia
Latin America & Caribbean
North America (excluding United States)
United States
Europe & Central Asia
East Asia & Pacific (excluding China)
China

Source: UNEP (database). https://unstats.un.org/sdgs/indicators/database?indicator=12.2.1

Adjusted net saving is a measure of economic sustainability. It monitors whether savings and investment compensate for depreciation and depletion of physical and natural capital and for pollution damages.

Share of gross national income, 2015 (%)

SDG 12.2

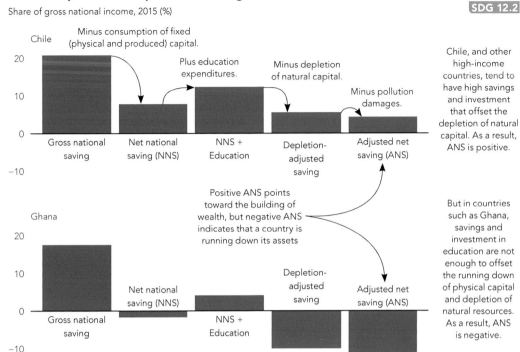

Chile

Minus consumption of fixed (physical and produced) capital.

Plus education expenditures.

Minus depletion of natural capital.

Minus pollution damages.

Gross national saving   Net national saving (NNS)   NNS + Education   Depletion-adjusted saving   Adjusted net saving (ANS)

Chile, and other high-income countries, tend to have high savings and investment that offset the depletion of natural capital. As a result, ANS is positive.

Ghana

Net national saving (NNS)   Depletion-adjusted saving   Adjusted net saving (ANS)

Gross national saving   NNS + Education

Positive ANS points toward the building of wealth, but negative ANS indicates that a country is running down its assets

But in countries such as Ghana, savings and investment in education are not enough to offset the running down of physical capital and depletion of natural resources. As a result, ANS is negative.

Source: World Bank and OECD. WDI (NY.ADJ.ICTR.GN.ZS; NY.ADJ.DKAP.GN.ZS; NY.ADJ.AEDU.GN.ZS; NY.ADJ.DFOR.GN.ZS; NY.ADJ.DNGY.GN.ZS; NY.ADJ.DMIN.GN.ZS; NY.ADJ.DCO2.GN.ZS; NY.ADJ.DPEM.GN.ZS).

Transforming natural resources into other forms of wealth is a major challenge. Many resource-rich low-income countries have negative adjusted net saving.

Adjusted net saving, average, 2010–16 (% of GNI)

SDG 12.2

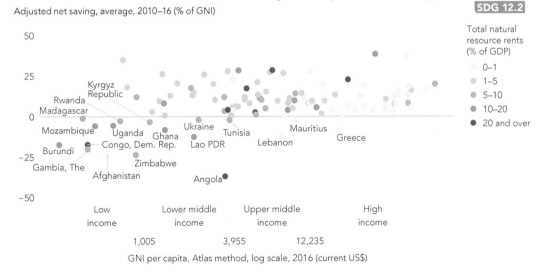

Total natural resource rents (% of GDP)

- 0–1
- 1–5
- 5–10
- 10–20
- 20 and over

Kyrgyz Republic
Rwanda
Madagascar
Mozambique
Uganda   Ghana
Congo, Dem. Rep.   Lao PDR
Burundi
Gambia, The
Zimbabwe
Afghanistan
Angola
Ukraine   Tunisia
Lebanon
Mauritius
Greece

Low income   Lower middle income   Upper middle income   High income

1,005   3,955   12,235

GNI per capita, Atlas method, log scale, 2016 (current US$)

Source: World Bank. World Development Indicators (NY.GNP.PCAP.CD; NY.ADJ.SVNG.GN.ZS; NY.GDP.TOTL.RT.ZS).

One-third of food produced for human consumption is lost or wasted. This is a waste of the resources used to produce, manage, and transport it.[a]

Food loss, 2013 (kilocalories per person per day)

SDG 12.3

Under 100   100–300   300 and over   No data

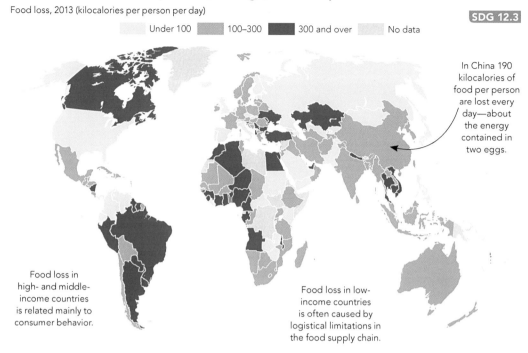

In China 190 kilocalories of food per person are lost every day—about the energy contained in two eggs.

Food loss in high- and middle-income countries is related mainly to consumer behavior.

Food loss in low-income countries is often caused by logistical limitations in the food supply chain.

a. FAO 2011 http://www.fao.org/docrep/014/mb060e/mb060e00.htm
Source: FAO Food Balance Sheets (database). http://www.fao.org/faostat/en/#data/FBS

The United States and China collect the most municipal waste, the majority of which makes its way to landfills.

Municipal waste, top 10 countries with data by total waste collected, most recent value in 2012–14

SDG 12.5

Landfill   Incinerate   Recycle   Compost   Unspecified

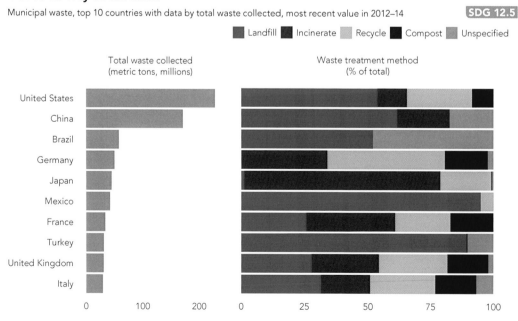

Total waste collected (metric tons, millions)

Waste treatment method (% of total)

Source: UNEP, UNSD (database). https://unstats.un.org/unsd/envstats/qindicators.cshtml

In two-thirds of countries for which there are data, over 50 percent of municipal waste goes to landfill. These statistics are still being developed by many countries.

Share of municipal waste that is sent to landfill, most recent value in 2012–14 (%)

0–25　　25–50　　50–75　　75–100　　No data　　SDG 12.5

Source: UNEP, UNSD (database). https://unstats.un.org/unsd/envstats/qindicators.cshtml

Only 1 in 10 countries with available data recycles or composts more than 50 percent of municipal waste.

Share of municipal waste that is recycled or composted, most recent value in 2012–14 (%)

0–1　　1–25　　25–50　　Over 50　　No data　　SDG 12.5

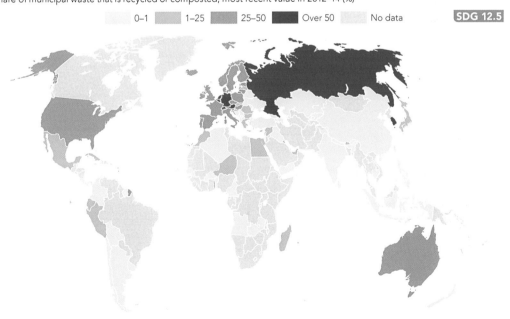

Source: UNEP, UNSD (database). https://unstats.un.org/unsd/envstats/qindicators.cshtml

Climate action*

Take urgent action to combat climate change and its impacts

13

Carbon dioxide (CO$_2$) emissions have been growing steadily...

Annual CO$_2$ emissions, by income group (Gt)

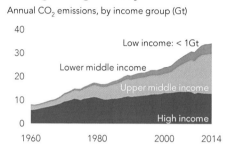

...so its concentration in the atmosphere is also growing—at an accelerating rate.

Atmospheric CO$_2$, at Mauna Loa, Hawaii (parts per million)

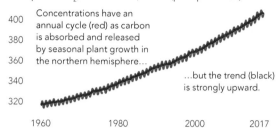

Concentrations have an annual cycle (red) as carbon is absorbed and released by seasonal plant growth in the northern hemisphere...

...but the trend (black) is strongly upward.

Source: Carbon Dioxide Information Analysis Center. World Development Indicators (EN.ATM.CO2E.KT).

Source: Tans, P / NOAA/ESRL & Keeling, R / Scripps Institution of Oceanography. http://www.esrl.noaa.gov/gmd/ccgg/trends

Climate change is caused by this atmospheric CO$_2$ and other greenhouse gases. Emissions per capita vary across and within income groups.

CO$_2$ emissions, by country and income group, 2014 (metric tons per capita)

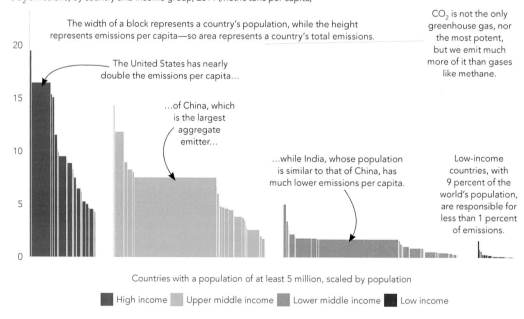

The width of a block represents a country's population, while the height represents emissions per capita—so area represents a country's total emissions.

The United States has nearly double the emissions per capita...

...of China, which is the largest aggregate emitter...

...while India, whose population is similar to that of China, has much lower emissions per capita.

CO$_2$ is not the only greenhouse gas, nor the most potent, but we emit much more of it than gases like methane.

Low-income countries, with 9 percent of the world's population, are responsible for less than 1 percent of emissions.

Countries with a population of at least 5 million, scaled by population

■ High income ■ Upper middle income ■ Lower middle income ■ Low income

Source: Carbon Dioxide Information Analysis Center. World Development Indicators (EN.ATM.CO2E.KT; SP.POP.TOTL).

* Acknowledging that the United Nations Framework Convention on Climate Change is the primary international, intergovernmental forum for negotiating the global response to climate change.

Further climate change is inevitable, but the degree of change depends on the path of future emissions of CO_2 and other greenhouse gases.

Annual CO_2 emissions, historical and four future scenarios used in climate modeling (Gt)

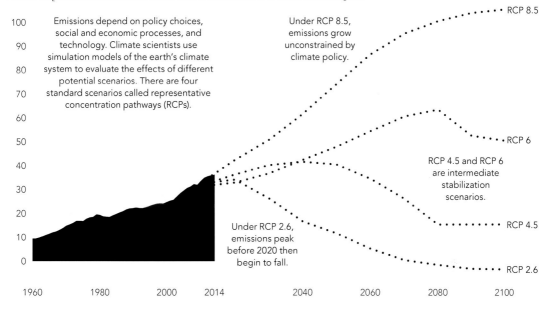

Emissions depend on policy choices, social and economic processes, and technology. Climate scientists use simulation models of the earth's climate system to evaluate the effects of different potential scenarios. There are four standard scenarios called representative concentration pathways (RCPs).

Under RCP 8.5, emissions grow unconstrained by climate policy.

RCP 4.5 and RCP 6 are intermediate stabilization scenarios.

Under RCP 2.6, emissions peak before 2020 then begin to fall.

Source: RCP Database (version 2.0.5). http://tntcat.iiasa.ac.at:8787/RcpDb

More frequent and intense extreme weather events are predicted, including extreme heat days, which threaten human health and agricultural productivity.

Annual additional days with heat index >35 degrees Celsius, projection for 2080–99, difference from 1986–2005

RCP 2.6 (low emissions)

RCP 8.5 (high emissions)

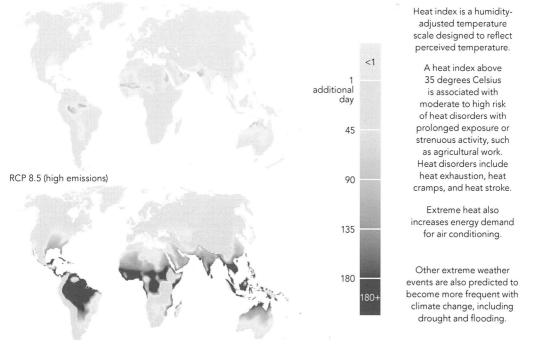

Heat index is a humidity-adjusted temperature scale designed to reflect perceived temperature.

A heat index above 35 degrees Celsius is associated with moderate to high risk of heat disorders with prolonged exposure or strenuous activity, such as agricultural work. Heat disorders include heat exhaustion, heat cramps, and heat stroke.

Extreme heat also increases energy demand for air conditioning.

Other extreme weather events are also predicted to become more frequent with climate change, including drought and flooding.

Note: CMIP5 Ensemble Model Projection.
Source: World Bank Climate Change Knowledge Portal. http://climateknowledgeportal.worldbank.org

Low-income countries tend to be more vulnerable to, and less equipped to invest against, extreme climate impacts.

Vulnerability to climate hazards, score, by country, 2016 (0–1, higher is more vulnerable)

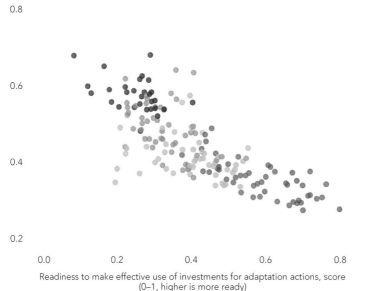

- Low income
- Lower middle income
- Upper middle income
- High income

Readiness to make effective use of investments for adaptation actions, score
(0–1, higher is more ready)

The Notre Dame-Global Adaptation Index is based on public data.

It measures vulnerability in six sectors: food, water, health, ecosystem service, human habitat, and infrastructure.

It measures readiness using three components: economic readiness, governance readiness and social readiness.

Source: Notre Dame Global Adaptation Initiative Country Index (database). https://gain.nd.edu/our-work/country-index

The risk to well-being from natural disasters is greater than narrow measures of asset loss suggest. The risk falls more heavily on the poor within countries.

Risk to well-being (% of GDP per year)

SDG 13.1

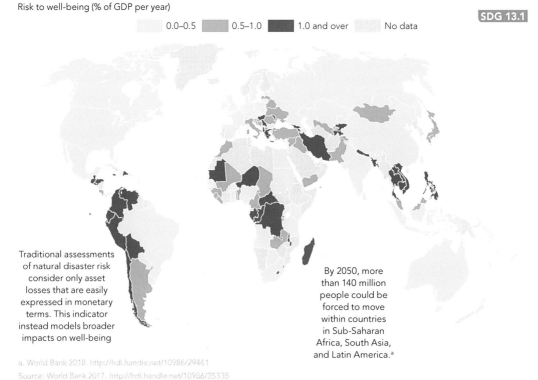

0.0–0.5   0.5–1.0   1.0 and over   No data

Traditional assessments of natural disaster risk consider only asset losses that are easily expressed in monetary terms. This indicator instead models broader impacts on well-being

By 2050, more than 140 million people could be forced to move within countries in Sub-Saharan Africa, South Asia, and Latin America.[a]

a. World Bank 2018. http://hdl.handle.net/10986/29461

Source: World Bank 2017. http://hdl.handle.net/10986/25335

Under the Paris Agreement, countries make commitments to reduce emissions (mitigation) and manage the adverse impacts of climate change (adaptation).

Number of countries with a commitment, by sector and income group

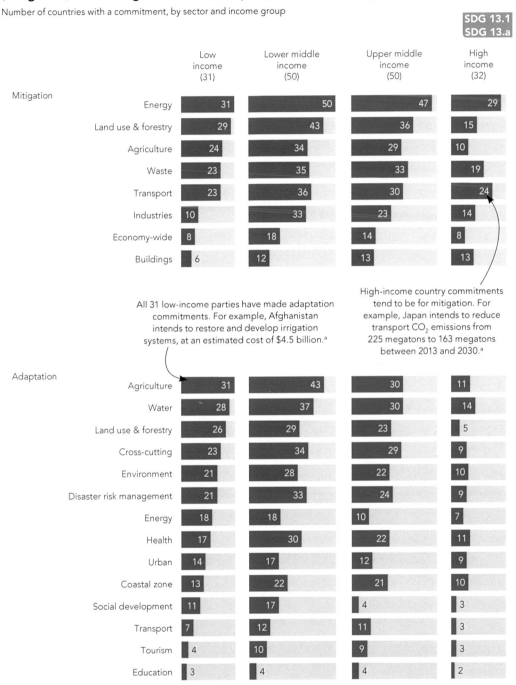

All 31 low-income parties have made adaptation commitments. For example, Afghanistan intends to restore and develop irrigation systems, at an estimated cost of $4.5 billion.[a]

High-income country commitments tend to be for mitigation. For example, Japan intends to reduce transport CO_2 emissions from 225 megatons to 163 megatons between 2013 and 2030.[a]

Many countries have not reported cost estimates for their commitments. For the 69 countries that have reported overall implementation cost estimates, the total is $5.2 trillion.

Note: Totals shown for each income group reflect the number of countries that have submitted Intended National Determine Contributions. As the European Union is a party to the agreement in its own right, it is counted as a single high-income country. a. UNFCCC NDC Registry (interim).
Source: World Bank Intended Nationally Determined Contributions (database). http://indc.worldbank.org

Life below water

Conserve and sustainably use the oceans, seas and marine resources for sustainable development

Industrial fishing takes place in more than half the world's ocean area, about four times the area of land-based agriculture.

Vessel-hours of fishing activity, 2016 (per sq. km)

SDG 14.4

This recently published dataset uses radio transmissions, emitted for collision avoidance, to track fishing vessels. It excludes small vessels and, probably, illegal fishing.

0	8.76	87.6	876 hours
	equivalent to 0.1%	1%	10% of a year

Each square kilometer of the most heavily fished regions of Europe and East Asia had activity equivalent to more than 10 percent of the 8,760 hours in a year.

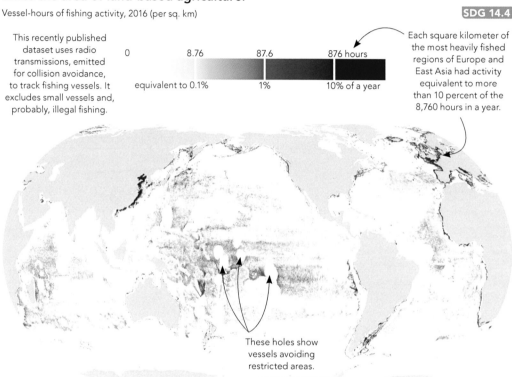

These holes show vessels avoiding restricted areas.

Source: Kroodsma and others 2018. http://doi.org/10.1126/science.aao5646

And 75 percent of fish catch is industrial.

Global fish catch (millions of metric tons)

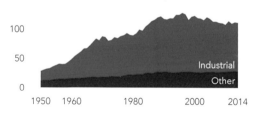

Note: "Other" includes subsistence, recreational, and artisanal sectors.
Source: Pauly and Zeller 2016. http://doi.org/10.1038/ncomms10244

Fish stocks are increasingly overfished.

State of global fish stocks (% of total stocks)

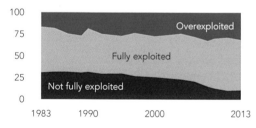

Source: FAO via UNSD Global SDG Indicators Database (14.4.1).

Activity on land can also damage seas. Hundreds of marine dead zones exist, with oxygen concentrations too low to support most life.

Marine dead zones, 2017 (count by hexagonal area)

SDG 14.1
SDG 14.2

0–4
5–9
10–29
30 and over

The northern Gulf of Mexico dead zone is the largest in the United States, measuring 22,000 square kilometers in 2017.

Dead zones occur primarily when fertilizer runoff enters the water. This promotes the growth of algae, which depletes the water of oxygen that more complex organisms need to live.

Source: Diaz and Rosenberg 2008, http://doi.org/10.1126/science.1156401. Current data at http://www.vims.edu/research/topics/dead_zones

Only about 7 percent of the world's ocean area is designated as marine protected area, officially reserved for long-term conservation.

Marine protected areas, 2018

SDG 14.5

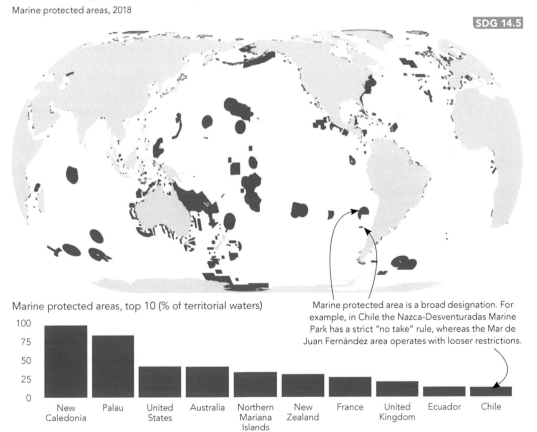

Marine protected areas, top 10 (% of territorial waters)

Marine protected area is a broad designation. For example, in Chile the Nazca-Desventuradas Marine Park has a strict "no take" rule, whereas the Mar de Juan Fernández area operates with looser restrictions.

100
75
50
25
0

New Caledonia
Palau
United States
Australia
Northern Mariana Islands
New Zealand
France
United Kingdom
Ecuador
Chile

Note: Excludes countries with less than 50,000 sq. km of protected area.

Source: UNEP–World Conservation Monitoring Centre Database on Protected Areas. WDI (ER.MRN.PTMR.ZS) and https://protectedplanet.net

Oceans are warmer because of climate change: sea surface temperature has increased in most places since 1901.

Change in sea surface temperature, 1901–2015 (degrees Celsius)

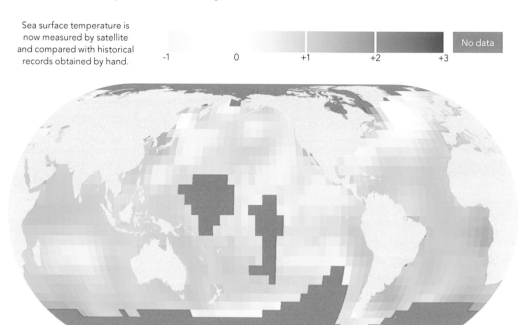

Sea surface temperature is now measured by satellite and compared with historical records obtained by hand.

-1   0   +1   +2   +3   No data

Average global sea surface temperature anomaly, relative to 1971–2000 average (degrees Celsius)

+0.5
1971–2000 average
0.0
−0.5
1900   1925   1950   1975   2000   2015

Source: U.S. Environmental Protection Agency. https://www.epa.gov/climate-indicators/climate-change-indicators-sea-surface-temperature

Warmer seas lead to coral bleaching or death, an outcome already observed in parts of Australia's Great Barrier Reef.

Average sea surface temperature anomaly, Great Barrier Reef, relative to 1961–90 average (degrees Celsius)

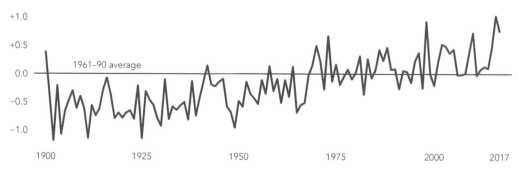

+1.0
+0.5
1961–90 average
0.0
−0.5
−1.0
1900   1925   1950   1975   2000   2017

Source: Australian Bureau of Meteorology. http://www.bom.gov.au/web01/ncc/www/cli_chg/timeseries/sst/0112/GBR/latest.txt

Marine organisms are also affected directly by atmospheric carbon dioxide, which dissolves in the oceans, raising acidity beyond safe levels.

Surface aragonite saturation state (Ω_{arg})

SDG 14.2

Aragonite is a mineral used in constructing the shells of marine organisms at the bottom of the food chain. When oceans acidify, aragonite cannot form and dissolves, threatening ecosystems and fisheries.

| Up to 1 | 1–2 | 2–3 | 3–4 | 4–5 |

Shells and coral skeletons begin to dissolve.

Organisms are stressed and may struggle to survive and reproduce.

Organisms can more easily build shells and skeletons. Above 4 is considered optimal.

2018

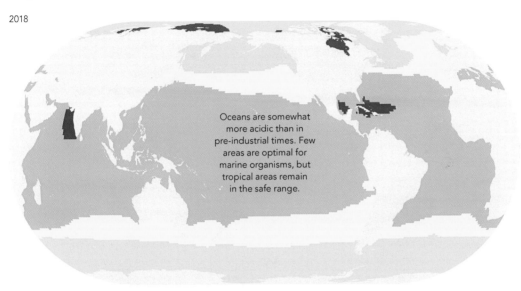

Oceans are somewhat more acidic than in pre-industrial times. Few areas are optimal for marine organisms, but tropical areas remain in the safe range.

2100, projected under RCP8.5 (high emissions) climate scenario (see page 51)

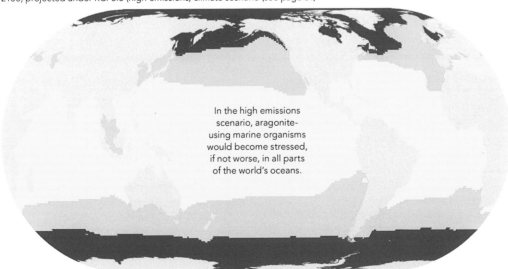

In the high emissions scenario, aragonite-using marine organisms would become stressed, if not worse, in all parts of the world's oceans.

Source: Friedrich, T. http://iprc.soest.hawaii.edu/users/tobiasf/Outreach/OA/Ocean_Acidification.html

Life on land

Protect, restore and promote sustainable use of
terrestrial ecosystems, sustainably manage forests,
combat desertification, and halt and reverse
land degradation and halt biodiversity loss

Most land is covered in vegetation. Forests dominate many regions.

Land cover, vegetation types, based on satellite imagery, 2015

SDG 15.1
SDG 15.2

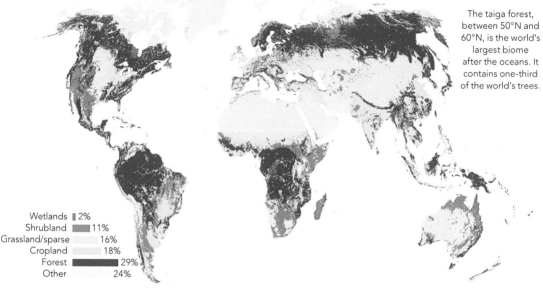

The taiga forest,
between 50°N and
60°N, is the world's
largest biome
after the oceans. It
contains one-third
of the world's trees.

Wetlands ▌2%
Shrubland �…11%
Grassland/sparse ▉ 16%
Cropland ▉ 18%
Forest ▉ 29%
Other 24%

Source: European Space Agency. https://www.esa-landcover-cci.org/?q=node/175

Just 10 countries account for two-thirds of global forest cover.

Forest area, by region with top 10 countries, 2015   SDG 15.2

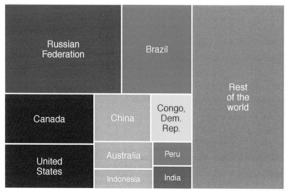

Source: FAO. WDI (AG.LND.FRST.K2).

Of these, only China's cover has been growing substantially.

Forest area, 1990 & 2015 (% of land area)

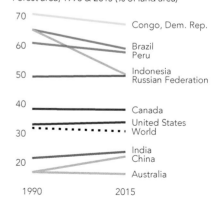

Source: FAO. WDI (AG.LND.FRST.ZS).

Some regions have experienced severe land degradation since 2000.

Change in net primary productivity, 2000-16 (grams of carbon per square meter per year)

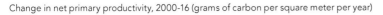

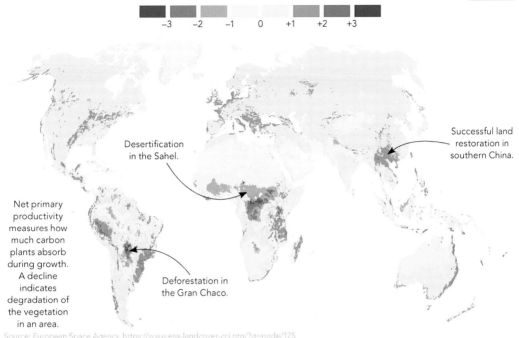

−3   −2   −1   0   +1   +2   +3

Desertification in the Sahel.

Successful land restoration in southern China.

Net primary productivity measures how much carbon plants absorb during growth. A decline indicates degradation of the vegetation in an area.

Deforestation in the Gran Chaco.

Source: European Space Agency. https://www.esa-landcover-cci.org/?q=node/175

Globally, about 14 percent of land is protected as national park, wildlife preserve, or a similar designation.

Terrestrial protected areas, 2016 (% of total land area)

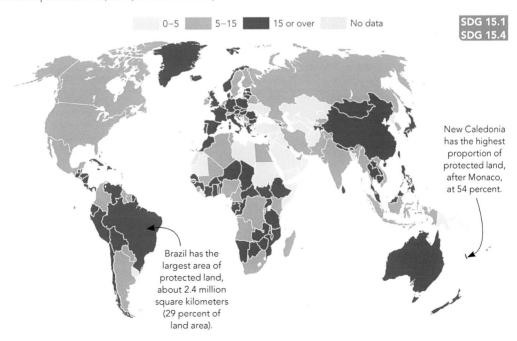

0–5   5–15   15 or over   No data

SDG 15.1
SDG 15.4

New Caledonia has the highest proportion of protected land, after Monaco, at 54 percent.

Brazil has the largest area of protected land, about 2.4 million square kilometers (29 percent of land area).

Source: UNEP, World Conservation Monitoring Centre, and WRI; WDI (ER.LND.PTLD.ZS).

Over half of assessed plant species and one-quarter of assessed animal species are threatened.

Threatened plant species, 2017 (% of all extant assessed plant species)

0–2   2–8   8–18   18 and over   No data

Species are assessed as threatened based on strict criteria including low population, reduction in population, limited habitat, and modeled extinction risk.

However, less than 10 percent of the estimated 391,000 plant species have been formally assessed.[a]

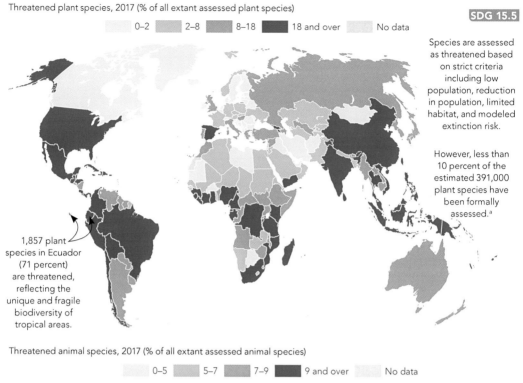

1,857 plant species in Ecuador (71 percent) are threatened, reflecting the unique and fragile biodiversity of tropical areas.

Threatened animal species, 2017 (% of all extant assessed animal species)

0–5   5–7   7–9   9 and over   No data

We know even less about animals than about plants. About 1 percent of the estimated 5 million land-based animal species have been assessed.[b]

1,050 animal species in the United States (16 percent) are threatened.

24 percent of animal species in Madagascar are threatened.

Note: Assumes data-deficient species are threatened in equal proportion to data-sufficient species. The proportion of threatened species can be larger for the world than for any country as threatened species, on average, exist in a smaller number of countries than nonthreatened species.
a. Royal Botanic Gardens Kew 2016, https://stateoftheworldsplants.com. b. Mora and others 2011, https://doi.org/10.1371/journal.pbio.1001127
Source: IUCN Red List of Threatened Species. http://http://www.iucnredlist.org

For some species, poaching is an existential threat. Commitments to tackling illegal wildlife trade in Africa and Asia totaled $1.3 billion between 2010 and 2016.

International donor commitments for combating illegal wildlife trade, 2010–16 (US$ millions)

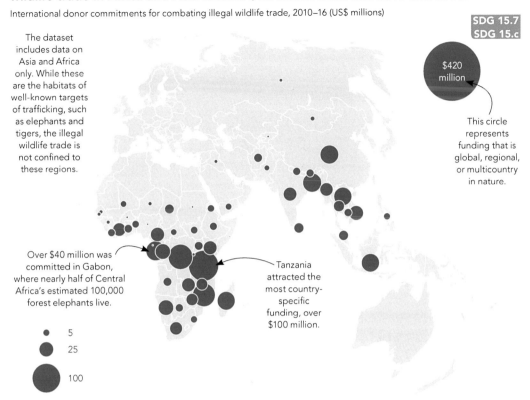

The dataset includes data on Asia and Africa only. While these are the habitats of well-known targets of trafficking, such as elephants and tigers, the illegal wildlife trade is not confined to these regions.

SDG 15.7
SDG 15.c

$420 million

This circle represents funding that is global, regional, or multicountry in nature.

Over $40 million was committed in Gabon, where nearly half of Central Africa's estimated 100,000 forest elephants live.

Tanzania attracted the most country-specific funding, over $100 million.

- 5
- 25
- 100

Source: World Bank 2016. http://hdl.handle.net/10986/25340

The largest category of funding for most countries is for the management of protected areas, to prevent poaching.

International donor commitments for combating illegal wildlife trade, top 19 recipient countries in Africa and Asia, 2010–16 (US$ millions)

SDG 15.7
SDG 15.c

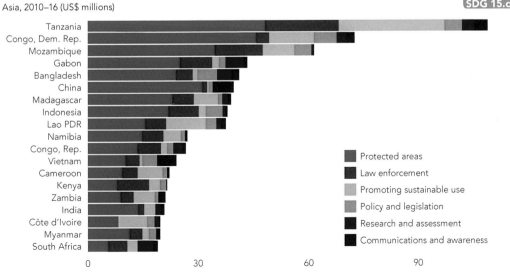

Legend:
- Protected areas
- Law enforcement
- Promoting sustainable use
- Policy and legislation
- Research and assessment
- Communications and awareness

Countries (top to bottom): Tanzania, Congo, Dem. Rep., Mozambique, Gabon, Bangladesh, China, Madagascar, Indonesia, Lao PDR, Namibia, Congo, Rep., Vietnam, Cameroon, Kenya, Zambia, India, Côte d'Ivoire, Myanmar, South Africa

X-axis: 0, 30, 60, 90

Source: World Bank 2016. http://hdl.handle.net/10986/25340

Peace, justice, and strong institutions

Promote peaceful and inclusive societies for sustainable development, provide access to justice for all, and build effective, accountable, and inclusive institutions at all levels

Homicide rates have declined dramatically in some countries.

Intentional homicides, five countries with largest reductions in rate (per 100,000 people)

SDG 16.1

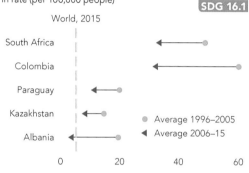

But battle-related deaths remain high because of the continuing Syrian conflict.

Battle-related deaths (thousands of people)

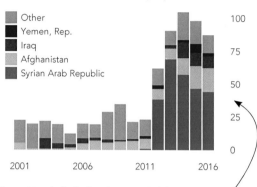

Source: UNODC. WDI (VC.IHR.PSRC.P5; SP.POP.TOTL).

Source: Uppsala Conflict Data Program. WDI (VC.BTL.DETH).

The World Bank currently identifies 36 fragile situations globally.

Fragile or conflict-affected situation

This indicator is a minimum estimate: it includes only reported deaths and excludes some categories of war deaths.

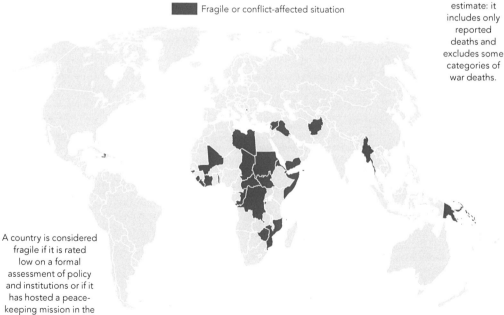

A country is considered fragile if it is rated low on a formal assessment of policy and institutions or if it has hosted a peace-keeping mission in the previous three years.

Source: World Bank. http://www.worldbank.org/en/topic/fragilityconflictviolence/brief/harmonized-list-of-fragile-situations

People often cross borders to seek refuge from conflict and fragility, but most remain in directly neighboring countries. Only a minority travel farther afield.

Refugees, by country of origin and country of asylum/residence, mid-2017

Country of origin

The top row represents the total number of refugees from each country of origin.

This circle represents the total global refugee population in mid-2017.

The right column represents the total number of refugees living in each country of asylum/residence.

18.5 million people

Country of asylum/residence

Afghanistan
Algeria
Austria
Bangladesh
Burundi
Cameroon
Canada
Chad
China
Congo, Dem. Rep.
Ecuador
Egypt, Arab Rep.
Ethiopia
France
Germany
India
Iran, Islamic Rep.
Iraq
Italy
Jordan
Kenya
Lebanon
Malaysia
Mauritania
Netherlands
Niger
Norway
Pakistan
Russian Federation
Rwanda
South Africa
South Sudan
Sudan
Sweden
Switzerland
Tanzania
Thailand
Turkey
Uganda
United Kingdom
United States
Venezuela, RB
Yemen, Rep.

Other countries

(Country of origin labels, left to right:)
Other countries
Afghanistan
Central African Republic
Burundi
China
Colombia
Congo, Dem. Rep.
Eritrea
Ethiopia
Iran, Islamic Rep.
Iraq
Mali
Myanmar
Nigeria
Pakistan
Russian Federation
Rwanda
Somalia
South Sudan
Sri Lanka
Sudan
Syrian Arab Republic
Turkey
Ukraine
Vietnam

Most of the 6 million refugees from Afghanistan are in Iran or Pakistan.

Refugees from the Syrian Arab Republic now total 6 million, about half of whom are in Turkey.

Turkey hosts 3.2 million refugees, the most of any destination country.

Note: "Other countries" includes countries and territories of origin or asylum/residence with a total refugee population of less than 50,000. Population is people reported by UNHCR to be refugees or in a refugee-like situation.

Source: UNHCR Population Statistics, mid-year 2017, version 3 (database). http://popstats.unhcr.org

A legal identity ensures basic human rights and allows participation in the formal economy. But registration at birth is often unavailable to the poor.

Completeness of birth registration, 40 countries with lowest registration in poorest quintile, most recent value in 2010–16 (%)

● Poorest quintile   ● Richest quintile

SDG 16.9

Birth registration is part of a complete civil registration system, in which the state formally records major life events including birth, death, marriage, and divorce.

Like the poor, refugees are particularly vulnerable to exclusion from civil registration—for example, children born to refugees may be ineligible for birth certificates in their host countries.

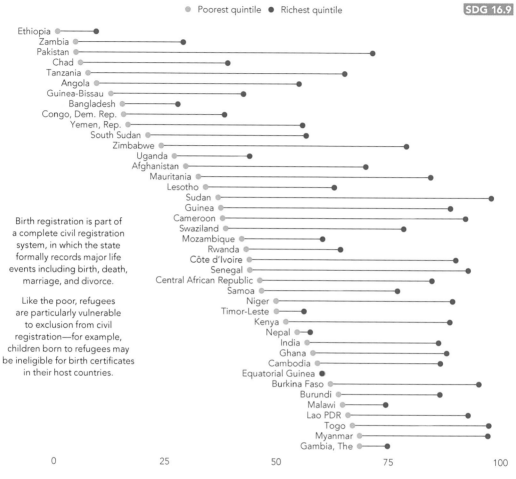

Source: UNICEF. Health Nutrition and Population Statistics by Wealth Quintile (SP.REG.BRTH.Q1.ZS; SP.REG.BRTH.Q5.ZS).

Corrupt public officials may make it harder for citizens and businesses to access government services.

Bribery and gifts (informal payments), 2016 (% of firms experiencing)

SDG 16.5

Note: Excludes data for most high-income countries. a. During six transactions dealing with utilities access, permits, licenses, and taxes.

Source: World Bank Enterprise Surveys. WDI (IC.FRM.BRIB.ZS; IC.FRM.CORR.ZS; IC.TAX.GIFT.ZS).

Public consultation in rule making protects the rule of law and provides a buffer against corruption.

Consolidated regulatory governance score, by country, 2016

SDG 16.6
SDG 16.7

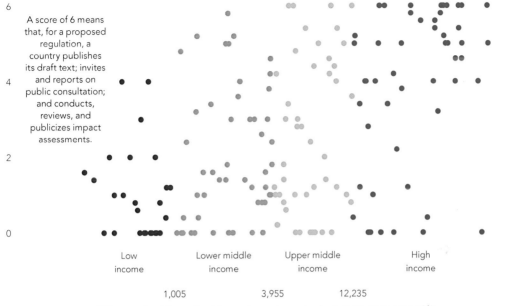

A score of 6 means that, for a proposed regulation, a country publishes its draft text; invites and reports on public consultation; and conducts, reviews, and publicizes impact assessments.

GNI per capita, Atlas method, log scale, most recent value in 2015–16 (current US$)

Source: World Bank Global Indicators of Regulatory Governance. World Development Indicators (NY.GNP.PCAP.CD).

Accountability also means setting, and sticking to, budgets for public expenditure.

Variation from the original approved budget expenditure, most recent value in 2007–17 (% above/below)

0–5   5–10   10–15   15 and over   No data

SDG 16.6

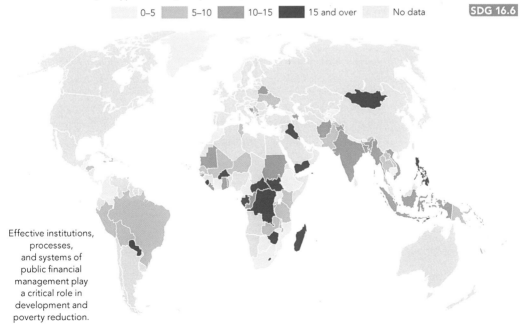

Effective institutions, processes, and systems of public financial management play a critical role in development and poverty reduction.

Source: Public Expenditure and Financial Accountability (database). https://pefa.org

Partnerships for the Goals

Strengthen the means of implementation and revitalize the global partnership for sustainable development

Official development assistance totaled $144 billion in 2016, but only six countries met the long-standing commitment to contribute 0.7 percent of GNI.

Official development assistance (ODA) from members of OECD's Development Assistance Committee, 2016   `SDG 17.2`

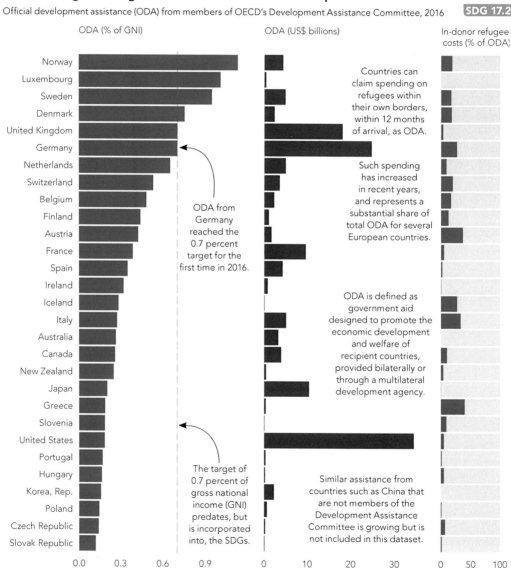

Source: OECD International Development Statistics (database). http://dx.doi.org/10.1787/dev-data-en

Loan disbursements from bilateral creditors (governments and their agencies) to low- and middle-income countries reached $54 billion in 2016, an all-time high.

Public and publicly guaranteed external debt, bilateral disbursements, 2016 (US$ billions)

SDG 17.3
SDG 17.4

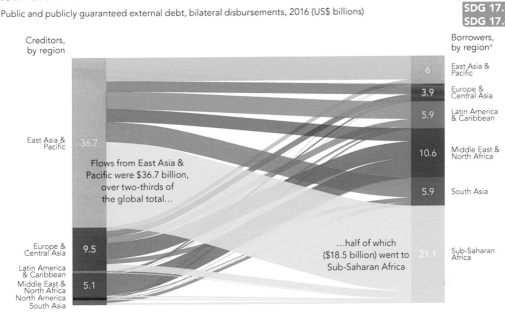

Note: Represents drawings by the borrower on bilateral debt, including loans from governments and their agencies (including central banks), loans from autonomous bodies, and direct loans from official export credit agencies. a. Excludes high-income countries.

Source: World Bank Debtor Reporting System. Aggregates by borrower available in World Development Indicators (DT.DIS.BLAT.CD).

Foreign direct investment and remittances to low- and middle-income countries totaled about $1 trillion in 2016.

Foreign direct investment, net inflows, and personal remittances, received (US$ billions)

SDG 17.3

— Foreign direct investment, net inflows   — Personal remittances, received

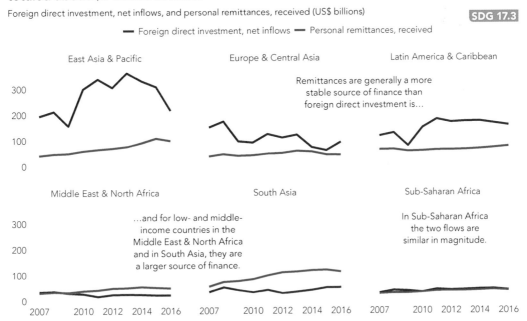

Note: Excludes high-income countries.

Source: World Bank, IMF, and UNCTAD. WDI (BX.KLT.DINV.CD.WD; BX.TRF.PWKR.CD.DT).

Exports can promote economic growth, but in many countries in Sub-Saharan Africa, firms tend to export little.

Proportion of total sales that are exported directly, manufacturing firms, most recent value in 2006–17 (%)

0–3   3–6   6 or over   No data   SDG 17.11

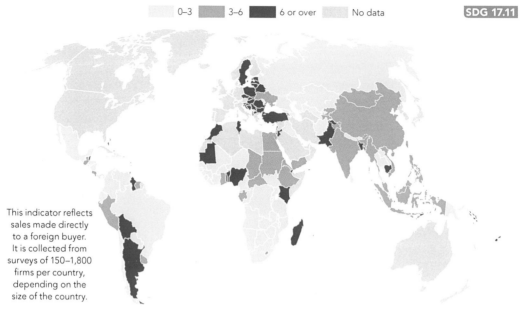

This indicator reflects sales made directly to a foreign buyer. It is collected from surveys of 150–1,800 firms per country, depending on the size of the country.

Source: World Bank. Enterprise Surveys (IC.FRM.TRD.TR5).

Engaging in international trade involves more barriers in low- and middle-income countries.

Ease of trading across borders, composite distance to frontier score, 2017 (0–100, higher is better)

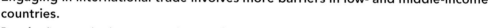

0–25   25–50   50–75   75–100   No data   SDG 17.11

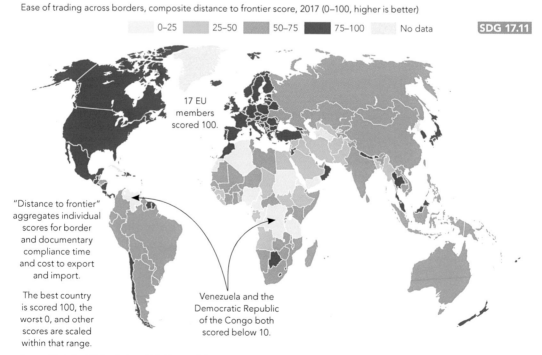

17 EU members scored 100.

"Distance to frontier" aggregates individual scores for border and documentary compliance time and cost to export and import.

The best country is scored 100, the worst 0, and other scores are scaled within that range.

Venezuela and the Democratic Republic of the Congo both scored below 10.

Source: World Bank Doing Business 2018 (database). http://www.doingbusiness.org

Public-private partnership investment, as a proportion of GDP, has declined in recent years.

Investment commitments in public-private partnerships, by target income group (% of GDP)

Note: Excludes information, communications, technology projects.
Source: World Bank Private Participation in Infrastructure (database). https://ppi.worldbank.org

Technology enables human development. In low-income countries only 12 percent of people use the Internet, but usage is growing.

Individuals using the Internet (% of population)

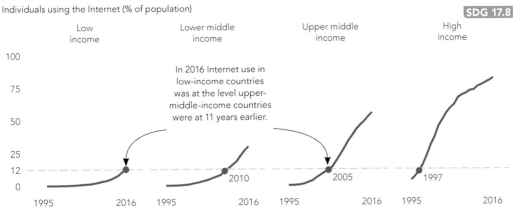

In 2016 Internet use in low-income countries was at the level upper-middle-income countries were at 11 years earlier.

Source: ITU. World Development Indicators (IT.NET.USER.ZS).

Fixed broadband Internet uptake is still negligible in Sub-Saharan Africa, but as mobile technology improves, this may not matter.

Subscriptions (per 100 people)

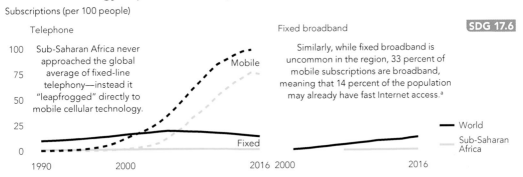

Sub-Saharan Africa never approached the global average of fixed-line telephony—instead it "leapfrogged" directly to mobile cellular technology.

Similarly, while fixed broadband is uncommon in the region, 33 percent of mobile subscriptions are broadband, meaning that 14 percent of the population may already have fast Internet access.[a]

a. GSMA 2017. https://www.gsma.com/mobileeconomy/sub-saharan-africa-2017/
Source: ITU. World Development Indicators (IT.NET.BBND.P2).

Sustainable Development Goals and targets

Goal 1 End poverty in all its forms everywhere

1.1 By 2030, eradicate extreme poverty for all people everywhere, currently measured as people living on less than $1.25 a day

1.2 By 2030, reduce at least by half the proportion of men, women and children of all ages living in poverty in all its dimensions according to national definitions

1.3 Implement nationally appropriate social protection systems and measures for all, including floors, and by 2030 achieve substantial coverage of the poor and the vulnerable

1.4 By 2030, ensure that all men and women, in particular the poor and the vulnerable, have equal rights to economic resources, as well as access to basic services, ownership and control over land and other forms of property, inheritance, natural resources, appropriate new technology and financial services, including microfinance

1.5 By 2030, build the resilience of the poor and those in vulnerable situations and reduce their exposure and vulnerability to climate-related extreme events and other economic, social and environmental shocks and disasters

1.a Ensure significant mobilization of resources from a variety of sources, including through enhanced development cooperation, in order to provide adequate and predictable means for developing countries, in particular least developed countries, to implement programmes and policies to end poverty in all its dimensions

1.b Create sound policy frameworks at the national, regional and international levels, based on pro-poor and gender-sensitive development strategies, to support accelerated investment in poverty eradication actions

Goal 2 End hunger, achieve food security and improved nutrition and promote sustainable agriculture

2.1 By 2030, end hunger and ensure access by all people, in particular the poor and people in vulnerable situations, including infants, to safe, nutritious and sufficient food all year round

2.2 By 2030, end all forms of malnutrition, including achieving, by 2025, the internationally agreed targets on stunting and wasting in children under 5 years of age, and address the nutritional needs of adolescent girls, pregnant and lactating women and older persons

2.3 By 2030, double the agricultural productivity and incomes of small-scale food producers, in particular women, indigenous peoples, family farmers, pastoralists and fishers, including through secure and equal access to land, other productive resources and inputs, knowledge, financial services, markets and opportunities for value addition and non-farm employment

2.4 By 2030, ensure sustainable food production systems and implement resilient agricultural practices that increase productivity and production, that help maintain ecosystems, that strengthen capacity for adaptation to climate change, extreme weather, drought, flooding and other disasters and that progressively improve land and soil quality

2.5 By 2020, maintain the genetic diversity of seeds, cultivated plants and farmed and domesticated animals and their related wild species, including through soundly managed and diversified seed and plant banks at the national, regional and international levels, and promote access to and fair and equitable sharing of benefits arising from the utilization of genetic resources and associated traditional knowledge, as internationally agreed

2.a Increase investment, including through enhanced international cooperation, in rural infrastructure, agricultural research and extension services, technology development and plant and livestock gene banks in order to enhance agricultural productive capacity in developing countries, in particular least developed countries

2.b Correct and prevent trade restrictions and distortions in world agricultural markets, including through the parallel elimination of all forms of agricultural export subsidies and all export measures with equivalent effect, in accordance with the mandate of the Doha Development Round

2.c Adopt measures to ensure the proper functioning of food commodity markets and their derivatives and facilitate timely access to market information, including on food reserves, in order to help limit extreme food price volatility

Goal 3 Ensure healthy lives and promote well-being for all at all ages

3.1 By 2030, reduce the global maternal mortality ratio to less than 70 per 100,000 live births

3.2 By 2030, end preventable deaths of newborns and children under 5 years of age, with all countries aiming to reduce neonatal mortality to at least as low as 12 per 1,000 live births and under-5 mortality to at least as low as 25 per 1,000 live births

3.3 By 2030, end the epidemics of AIDS, tuberculosis, malaria and neglected tropical diseases and combat hepatitis, water-borne diseases and other communicable diseases

3.4 By 2030, reduce by one third premature mortality from non-communicable diseases through prevention and treatment and promote mental health and well-being

3.5 Strengthen the prevention and treatment of substance abuse, including narcotic drug abuse and harmful use of alcohol

3.6 By 2020, halve the number of global deaths and injuries from road traffic accidents

3.7　By 2030, ensure universal access to sexual and reproductive health-care services, including for family planning, information and education, and the integration of reproductive health into national strategies and programmes

3.8　Achieve universal health coverage, including financial risk protection, access to quality essential health-care services and access to safe, effective, quality and affordable essential medicines and vaccines for all

3.9　By 2030, substantially reduce the number of deaths and illnesses from hazardous chemicals and air, water and soil pollution and contamination

3.a　Strengthen the implementation of the World Health Organization Framework Convention on Tobacco Control in all countries, as appropriate

3.b　Support the research and development of vaccines and medicines for the communicable and non-communicable diseases that primarily affect developing countries, provide access to affordable essential medicines and vaccines, in accordance with the Doha Declaration on the TRIPS Agreement and Public Health, which affirms the right of developing countries to use to the full the provisions in the Agreement on Trade-Related Aspects of Intellectual Property Rights regarding flexibilities to protect public health, and, in particular, provide access to medicines for all

3.c　Substantially increase health financing and the recruitment, development, training and retention of the health workforce in developing countries, especially in least developed countries and small island developing States

3.d　Strengthen the capacity of all countries, in particular developing countries, for early warning, risk reduction and management of national and global health risks

Goal 4　Ensure inclusive and equitable quality education and promote lifelong learning opportunities for all

4.1　By 2030, ensure that all girls and boys complete free, equitable and quality primary and secondary education leading to relevant and effective learning outcomes

4.2　By 2030, ensure that all girls and boys have access to quality early childhood development, care and pre-primary education so that they are ready for primary education

4.3　By 2030, ensure equal access for all women and men to affordable and quality technical, vocational and tertiary education, including university

4.4　By 2030, substantially increase the number of youth and adults who have relevant skills, including technical and vocational skills, for employment, decent jobs and entrepreneurship

4.5　By 2030, eliminate gender disparities in education and ensure equal access to all levels of education and vocational training for the vulnerable, including persons with disabilities, indigenous peoples and children in vulnerable situations

4.6　By 2030, ensure that all youth and a substantial proportion of adults, both men and women, achieve literacy and numeracy

4.7　By 2030, ensure that all learners acquire the knowledge and skills needed to promote sustainable development, including, among others, through education for sustainable development and sustainable lifestyles, human rights, gender equality, promotion of a culture of peace and non-violence, global citizenship and appreciation of cultural diversity and of culture's contribution to sustainable development

4.a　Build and upgrade education facilities that are child, disability and gender sensitive and provide safe, non-violent, inclusive and effective learning environments for all

4.b　By 2020, substantially expand globally the number of scholarships available to developing countries, in particular least developed countries, small island developing States and African countries, for enrolment in higher education, including vocational training and information and communications technology, technical, engineering and scientific programmes, in developed countries and other developing countries

4.c　By 2030, substantially increase the supply of qualified teachers, including through international cooperation for teacher training in developing countries, especially least developed countries and small island developing States

Goal 5　Achieve gender equality and empower all women and girls

5.1　End all forms of discrimination against all women and girls everywhere

5.2　Eliminate all forms of violence against all women and girls in the public and private spheres, including trafficking and sexual and other types of exploitation

5.3　Eliminate all harmful practices, such as child, early and forced marriage and female genital mutilation

5.4　Recognize and value unpaid care and domestic work through the provision of public services, infrastructure and social protection policies and the promotion of shared responsibility within the household and the family as nationally appropriate

5.5　Ensure women's full and effective participation and equal opportunities for leadership at all levels of decision-making in political, economic and public life

5.6　Ensure universal access to sexual and reproductive health and reproductive rights as agreed in accordance with the Programme of Action of the International Conference on Population and Development and the Beijing Platform for Action and the outcome documents of their review conferences

5.a　Undertake reforms to give women equal rights to economic resources, as well as access to ownership and control over land and other forms of property, financial services, inheritance and natural resources, in accordance with national laws

5.b　Enhance the use of enabling technology, in particular information and communications technology, to promote the empowerment of women

5.c　Adopt and strengthen sound policies and enforceable legislation for the promotion of gender equality and the empowerment of all women and girls at all levels

Goal 6 Ensure availability and sustainable management of water and sanitation for all

6.1 By 2030, achieve universal and equitable access to safe and affordable drinking water for all

6.2 By 2030, achieve access to adequate and equitable sanitation and hygiene for all and end open defecation, paying special attention to the needs of women and girls and those in vulnerable situations

6.3 By 2030, improve water quality by reducing pollution, eliminating dumping and minimizing release of hazardous chemicals and materials, halving the proportion of untreated wastewater and substantially increasing recycling and safe reuse globally

6.4 By 2030, substantially increase water-use efficiency across all sectors and ensure sustainable withdrawals and supply of freshwater to address water scarcity and substantially reduce the number of people suffering from water scarcity

6.5 By 2030, implement integrated water resources management at all levels, including through transboundary cooperation as appropriate

6.6 By 2020, protect and restore water-related ecosystems, including mountains, forests, wetlands, rivers, aquifers and lakes

6.a By 2030, expand international cooperation and capacity-building support to developing countries in water- and sanitation-related activities and programmes, including water harvesting, desalination, water efficiency, wastewater treatment, recycling and reuse technologies

6.b Support and strengthen the participation of local communities in improving water and sanitation management

Goal 7 Ensure access to affordable, reliable, sustainable and modern energy for all

7.1 By 2030, ensure universal access to affordable, reliable and modern energy services

7.2 By 2030, increase substantially the share of renewable energy in the global energy mix

7.3 By 2030, double the global rate of improvement in energy efficiency

7.a By 2030, enhance international cooperation to facilitate access to clean energy research and technology, including renewable energy, energy efficiency and advanced and cleaner fossil-fuel technology, and promote investment in energy infrastructure and clean energy technology

7.b By 2030, expand infrastructure and upgrade technology for supplying modern and sustainable energy services for all in developing countries, in particular least developed countries, small island developing States and landlocked developing countries, in accordance with their respective programmes of support

Goal 8 Promote sustained, inclusive and sustainable economic growth, full and productive employment and decent work for all

8.1 Sustain per capita economic growth in accordance with national circumstances and, in particular, at least 7 percent gross domestic product growth per annum in the least developed countries

8.2 Achieve higher levels of economic productivity through diversification, technological upgrading and innovation, including through a focus on high-value added and labour-intensive sectors

8.3 Promote development-oriented policies that support productive activities, decent job creation, entrepreneurship, creativity and innovation, and encourage the formalization and growth of micro-, small- and medium-sized enterprises, including through access to financial services

8.4 Improve progressively, through 2030, global resource efficiency in consumption and production and endeavour to decouple economic growth from environmental degradation, in accordance with the 10-Year Framework of Programmes on Sustainable Consumption and Production, with developed countries taking the lead

8.5 By 2030, achieve full and productive employment and decent work for all women and men, including for young people and persons with disabilities, and equal pay for work of equal value

8.6 By 2020, substantially reduce the proportion of youth not in employment, education or training

8.7 Take immediate and effective measures to eradicate forced labour, end modern slavery and human trafficking and secure the prohibition and elimination of the worst forms of child labour, including recruitment and use of child soldiers, and by 2025 end child labour in all its forms

8.8 Protect labour rights and promote safe and secure working environments for all workers, including migrant workers, in particular women migrants, and those in precarious employment

8.9 By 2030, devise and implement policies to promote sustainable tourism that creates jobs and promotes local culture and products

8.10 Strengthen the capacity of domestic financial institutions to encourage and expand access to banking, insurance and financial services for all

8.a Increase Aid for Trade support for developing countries, in particular least developed countries, including through the Enhanced Integrated Framework for Trade-related Technical Assistance to Least Developed Countries

8.b By 2020, develop and operationalize a global strategy for youth employment and implement the Global Jobs Pact of the International Labour Organization

Goal 9 Build resilient infrastructure, promote inclusive and sustainable industrialization and foster innovation

9.1 Develop quality, reliable, sustainable and resilient infrastructure, including regional and transborder infrastructure, to support economic development and human well-being, with a focus on affordable and equitable access for all

9.2 Promote inclusive and sustainable industrialization and, by 2030, significantly raise industry's share of employment and gross domestic product, in line with national circumstances, and double its share in least developed countries

9.3 Increase the access of small-scale industrial and other enterprises, in particular in developing countries, to financial services, including affordable credit, and their integration into value chains and markets

9.4 By 2030, upgrade infrastructure and retrofit industries to make them sustainable, with increased resource-use efficiency and greater adoption of clean and environmentally sound technologies and industrial processes, with all countries taking action in accordance with their respective capabilities

9.5 Enhance scientific research, upgrade the technological capabilities of industrial sectors in all countries, in particular developing countries, including, by 2030, encouraging innovation and substantially increasing the number of research and development workers per 1 million people and public and private research and development spending

9.a Facilitate sustainable and resilient infrastructure development in developing countries through enhanced financial, technological and technical support to African countries, least developed countries, landlocked developing countries and small island developing States

9.b Support domestic technology development, research and innovation in developing countries, including by ensuring a conducive policy environment for, inter alia, industrial diversification and value addition to commodities

9.c Significantly increase access to information and communications technology and strive to provide universal and affordable access to the Internet in least developed countries by 2020

Goal 10 Reduce inequality within and among countries

10.1 By 2030, progressively achieve and sustain income growth of the bottom 40 percent of the population at a rate higher than the national average

10.2 By 2030, empower and promote the social, economic and political inclusion of all, irrespective of age, sex, disability, race, ethnicity, origin, religion or economic or other status

10.3 Ensure equal opportunity and reduce inequalities of outcome, including by eliminating discriminatory laws, policies and practices and promoting appropriate legislation, policies and action in this regard

10.4 Adopt policies, especially fiscal, wage and social protection policies, and progressively achieve greater equality

10.5 Improve the regulation and monitoring of global financial markets and institutions and strengthen the implementation of such regulations

10.6 Ensure enhanced representation and voice for developing countries in decision-making in global international economic and financial institutions in order to deliver more effective, credible, accountable and legitimate institutions

10.7 Facilitate orderly, safe, regular and responsible migration and mobility of people, including through the implementation of planned and well-managed migration policies

10.a Implement the principle of special and differential treatment for developing countries, in particular least developed countries, in accordance with World Trade Organization agreements

10.b Encourage official development assistance and financial flows, including foreign direct investment, to States where the need is greatest, in particular least developed countries, African countries, small island developing States and landlocked developing countries, in accordance with their national plans and programmes

10.c By 2030, reduce to less than 3 percent the transaction costs of migrant remittances and eliminate remittance corridors with costs higher than 5 percent

Goal 11 Make cities and human settlements inclusive, safe, resilient and sustainable

11.1 By 2030, ensure access for all to adequate, safe and affordable housing and basic services and upgrade slums

11.2 By 2030, provide access to safe, affordable, accessible and sustainable transport systems for all, improving road safety, notably by expanding public transport, with special attention to the needs of those in vulnerable situations, women, children, persons with disabilities and older persons

11.3 By 2030, enhance inclusive and sustainable urbanization and capacity for participatory, integrated and sustainable human settlement planning and management in all countries

11.4 Strengthen efforts to protect and safeguard the world's cultural and natural heritage

11.5 By 2030, significantly reduce the number of deaths and the number of people affected and substantially decrease the direct economic losses relative to global gross domestic product caused by disasters, including water-related disasters, with a focus on protecting the poor and people in vulnerable situations

11.6 By 2030, reduce the adverse per capita environmental impact of cities, including by paying special attention to air quality and municipal and other waste management

11.7 By 2030, provide universal access to safe, inclusive and accessible, green and public spaces, in particular for women and children, older persons and persons with disabilities

11.a Support positive economic, social and environmental links between urban, peri-urban and rural areas by strengthening national and regional development planning

11.b By 2020, substantially increase the number of cities and human settlements adopting and implementing integrated policies and plans towards inclusion, resource efficiency, mitigation and adaptation to climate change, resilience to disasters, and develop and implement, in line with the Sendai Framework for Disaster Risk Reduction 2015–2030, holistic disaster risk management at all levels

11.c Support least developed countries, including through financial and technical assistance, in building sustainable and resilient buildings utilizing local materials

Goal 12 Ensure sustainable consumption and production patterns

12.1 Implement the 10-Year Framework of Programmes on Sustainable Consumption and Production Patterns, all countries taking action, with developed countries taking the lead, taking into account the development and capabilities of developing countries

12.2 By 2030, achieve the sustainable management and efficient use of natural resources

12.3 By 2030, halve per capita global food waste at the retail and consumer levels and reduce food losses along production and supply chains, including post-harvest losses

12.4 By 2020, achieve the environmentally sound management of chemicals and all wastes throughout their life cycle, in accordance with agreed international frameworks, and significantly reduce their release to air, water and soil in order to minimize their adverse impacts on human health and the environment

12.5 By 2030, substantially reduce waste generation through prevention, reduction, recycling and reuse

12.6 Encourage companies, especially large and transnational companies, to adopt sustainable practices and to integrate sustainability information into their reporting cycle

12.7 Promote public procurement practices that are sustainable, in accordance with national policies and priorities

12.8 By 2030, ensure that people everywhere have the relevant information and awareness for sustainable development and lifestyles in harmony with nature

12.a Support developing countries to strengthen their scientific and technological capacity to move towards more sustainable patterns of consumption and production

12.b Develop and implement tools to monitor sustainable development impacts for sustainable tourism that creates jobs and promotes local culture and products

12.c Rationalize inefficient fossil-fuel subsidies that encourage wasteful consumption by removing market distortions, in accordance with national circumstances, including by restructuring taxation and phasing out those harmful subsidies, where they exist, to reflect their environmental impacts, taking fully into account the specific needs and conditions of developing countries and minimizing the possible adverse impacts on their development in a manner that protects the poor and the affected communities

Goal 13 Take urgent action to combat climate change and its impacts*

13.1 Strengthen resilience and adaptive capacity to climate-related hazards and natural disasters in all countries

13.2 Integrate climate change measures into national policies, strategies and planning

13.3 Improve education, awareness-raising and human and institutional capacity on climate change mitigation, adaptation, impact reduction and early warning

13.a Implement the commitment undertaken by developed-country parties to the United Nations Framework Convention on Climate Change to a goal of mobilizing jointly $100 billion annually by 2020 from all sources to address the needs of developing countries in the context of meaningful mitigation actions and transparency on implementation and fully operationalize the Green Climate Fund through its capitalization as soon as possible

13.b Promote mechanisms for raising capacity for effective climate change-related planning and management in least developed countries and small island developing States, including focusing on women, youth and local and marginalized communities

Goal 14 Conserve and sustainably use the oceans, seas and marine resources for sustainable development

14.1 By 2025, prevent and significantly reduce marine pollution of all kinds, in particular from land-based activities, including marine debris and nutrient pollution

14.2 By 2020, sustainably manage and protect marine and coastal ecosystems to avoid significant adverse impacts, including by strengthening their resilience, and take action for their restoration in order to achieve healthy and productive oceans

14.3 Minimize and address the impacts of ocean acidification, including through enhanced scientific cooperation at all levels

14.4 By 2020, effectively regulate harvesting and end overfishing, illegal, unreported and unregulated fishing and destructive fishing practices and implement science-based management plans, in order to restore fish stocks in the shortest time feasible, at least to levels that can produce maximum sustainable yield as determined by their biological characteristics

14.5 By 2020, conserve at least 10 percent of coastal and marine areas, consistent with national and international law and based on the best available scientific information

14.6 By 2020, prohibit certain forms of fisheries subsidies which contribute to overcapacity and overfishing, eliminate subsidies that contribute to illegal, unreported and unregulated fishing and refrain from introducing new such subsidies, recognizing that appropriate and effective special and differential treatment for developing and least developed countries should be an integral part of the World Trade Organization fisheries subsidies negotiation

* Acknowledging that the United Nations Framework Convention on Climate Change is the primary international, intergovernmental forum for negotiating the global response to climate change.

14.7 By 2030, increase the economic benefits to small island developing States and least developed countries from the sustainable use of marine resources, including through sustainable management of fisheries, aquaculture and tourism

14.a Increase scientific knowledge, develop research capacity and transfer marine technology, taking into account the Intergovernmental Oceanographic Commission Criteria and Guidelines on the Transfer of Marine Technology, in order to improve ocean health and to enhance the contribution of marine biodiversity to the development of developing countries, in particular small island developing States and least developed countries

14.b Provide access for small-scale artisanal fishers to marine resources and markets

14.c Enhance the conservation and sustainable use of oceans and their resources by implementing international law as reflected in the United Nations Convention on the Law of the Sea, which provides the legal framework for the conservation and sustainable use of oceans and their resources, as recalled in paragraph 158 of "The future we want"

Goal 15 Protect, restore and promote sustainable use of terrestrial ecosystems, sustainably manage forests, combat desertification, and halt and reverse land degradation and halt biodiversity loss

15.1 By 2020, ensure the conservation, restoration and sustainable use of terrestrial and inland freshwater ecosystems and their services, in particular forests, wetlands, mountains and drylands, in line with obligations under international agreements

15.2 By 2020, promote the implementation of sustainable management of all types of forests, halt deforestation, restore degraded forests and substantially increase afforestation and reforestation globally

15.3 By 2030, combat desertification, restore degraded land and soil, including land affected by desertification, drought and floods, and strive to achieve a land degradation-neutral world

15.4 By 2030, ensure the conservation of mountain ecosystems, including their biodiversity, in order to enhance their capacity to provide benefits that are essential for sustainable development

15.5 Take urgent and significant action to reduce the degradation of natural habitats, halt the loss of biodiversity and, by 2020, protect and prevent the extinction of threatened species

15.6 Promote fair and equitable sharing of the benefits arising from the utilization of genetic resources and promote appropriate access to such resources, as internationally agreed

15.7 Take urgent action to end poaching and trafficking of protected species of flora and fauna and address both demand and supply of illegal wildlife products

15.8 By 2020, introduce measures to prevent the introduction and significantly reduce the impact of invasive alien species on land and water ecosystems and control or eradicate the priority species

15.9 By 2020, integrate ecosystem and biodiversity values into national and local planning, development processes, poverty reduction strategies and accounts

15.a Mobilize and significantly increase financial resources from all sources to conserve and sustainably use biodiversity and ecosystems

15.b Mobilize significant resources from all sources and at all levels to finance sustainable forest management and provide adequate incentives to developing countries to advance such management, including for conservation and reforestation

15.c Enhance global support for efforts to combat poaching and trafficking of protected species, including by increasing the capacity of local communities to pursue sustainable livelihood opportunities

Goal 16 Promote peaceful and inclusive societies for sustainable development, provide access to justice for all and build effective, accountable and inclusive institutions at all levels

16.1 Significantly reduce all forms of violence and related death rates everywhere

16.2 End abuse, exploitation, trafficking and all forms of violence against and torture of children

16.3 Promote the rule of law at the national and international levels and ensure equal access to justice for all

16.4 By 2030, significantly reduce illicit financial and arms flows, strengthen the recovery and return of stolen assets and combat all forms of organized crime

16.5 Substantially reduce corruption and bribery in all their forms

16.6 Develop effective, accountable and transparent institutions at all levels

16.7 Ensure responsive, inclusive, participatory and representative decision-making at all levels

16.8 Broaden and strengthen the participation of developing countries in the institutions of global governance

16.9 By 2030, provide legal identity for all, including birth registration

16.10 Ensure public access to information and protect fundamental freedoms, in accordance with national legislation and international agreements

16.a Strengthen relevant national institutions, including through international cooperation, for building capacity at all levels, in particular in developing countries, to prevent violence and combat terrorism and crime

16.b Promote and enforce non-discriminatory laws and policies for sustainable development

Goal 17 Strengthen the means of implementation and revitalize the global partnership for sustainable development

17.1 Strengthen domestic resource mobilization, including through international support to developing countries, to improve domestic capacity for tax and other revenue collection

17.2 Developed countries to implement fully their official development assistance commitments, including the commitment by many developed countries to achieve the target of 0.7 per cent of gross national income for official development assistance (ODA/GNI) to developing countries and 0.15 to 0.20 per cent of ODA/GNI to least developed countries; ODA providers are encouraged to consider setting a target to provide at least 0.20 per cent of ODA/GNI to least developed countries

17.3 Mobilize additional financial resources for developing countries from multiple sources

17.4 Assist developing countries in attaining long-term debt sustainability through coordinated policies aimed at fostering debt financing, debt relief and debt restructuring, as appropriate, and address the external debt of highly indebted poor countries to reduce debt distress

17.5 Adopt and implement investment promotion regimes for least developed countries

17.6 Enhance North-South, South-South and triangular regional and international cooperation on and access to science, technology and innovation and enhance knowledge-sharing on mutually agreed terms, including through improved coordination among existing mechanisms, in particular at the United Nations level, and through a global technology facilitation mechanism

17.7 Promote the development, transfer, dissemination and diffusion of environmentally sound technologies to developing countries on favourable terms, including on concessional and preferential terms, as mutually agreed

17.8 Fully operationalize the technology bank and science, technology and innovation capacity-building mechanism for least developed countries by 2017 and enhance the use of enabling technology, in particular information and communications technology

17.9 Enhance international support for implementing effective and targeted capacity-building in developing countries to support national plans to implement all the Sustainable Development Goals, including through North-South, South-South and triangular cooperation

17.10 Promote a universal, rules-based, open, non-discriminatory and equitable multilateral trading system under the World Trade Organization, including through the conclusion of negotiations under its Doha Development Agenda

17.11 Significantly increase the exports of developing countries, in particular with a view to doubling the least developed countries' share of global exports by 2020

17.12 Realize timely implementation of duty-free and quota-free market access on a lasting basis for all least developed countries, consistent with World Trade Organization decisions, including by ensuring that preferential rules of origin applicable to imports from least developed countries are transparent and simple, and contribute to facilitating market access

17.13 Enhance global macroeconomic stability, including through policy coordination and policy coherence

17.14 Enhance policy coherence for sustainable development

17.15 Respect each country's policy space and leadership to establish and implement policies for poverty eradication and sustainable development

17.16 Enhance the Global Partnership for Sustainable Development, complemented by multi-stakeholder partnerships that mobilize and share knowledge, expertise, technology and financial resources, to support the achievement of the Sustainable Development Goals in all countries, in particular developing countries

17.17 Encourage and promote effective public, public-private and civil society partnerships, building on the experience and resourcing strategies of partnerships

17.18 By 2020, enhance capacity-building support to developing countries, including for least developed countries and small island developing States, to increase significantly the availability of high-quality, timely and reliable data disaggregated by income, gender, age, race, ethnicity, migratory status, disability, geographic location and other characteristics relevant in national contexts

17.19 By 2030, build on existing initiatives to develop measurements of progress on sustainable development that complement gross domestic product, and support statistical capacity-building in developing countries